# A TASTE OF

# AFRICA

With over 100 traditional African recipes
adapted for the modern cook

# A TASTE OF AFRICA

With over 100 traditional African recipes
adapted for the modern cook

# DORINDA HAFNER

TEN SPEED PRESS
Berkeley, California

*For Elizabeth*
*thank you mother*
*'okortor nwo anoma'*
*'kaa for loo flor'*

*For my children*
*James and Nuala*
*'a crab cannot produce a bird'*

*For the many women, quiet achievers*
*'esie ne kegya nni aseda'*
*'wuor ker tumo ber shidaa'*

A TASTE OF AFRICA

First published in Australasia in 1993 by
Simon & Schuster Australia
20 Barcoo Street, East Roseville NSW 2069

Photographs © 1993 Simon & Schuster Australia
Text and cover design by Jack Jagtenberg
Photography by Jonathan Chester/Extreme Images
Maps by Greg Campbell/Greg Campbell Design
Illustrations by Skye Rogers
Typesetting by The Type House, Sydney
Produced by Mandarin Offset in Hong Kong

Ten Speed Press
P.O. Box 7123
Berkeley, California 94707
FIRST TEN SPEED PRESS PRINTING 1993

Library of Congress Cataloguing in Publication Data

Hafner, Dorinda.
A taste of Africa / Dorinda Hafner.
p.   cm.
Includes bibliographical reference and index.
ISBN 0-89815-522-3
1. Cookery, African. 2. Africa—Social life and customs.
I. Title.
TX7825.A4H35    1982
641.596--dc20

Printed in Hong Kong
1  2  3  4  5 — 96  95  94  93  92

The television series, *A Taste of Africa*,
has been sponsored by Air Zimbabwe

# CONTENTS

# ACKNOWLEDGEMENTS

To the following people I give my most heartfelt thanks:

Alex Moshe (Tanzania)   I can now boast of more than two words of Swahili Thanks.

Annette Holton (Trinidad and Tobago)   Your recipes are as hybrid and rich as yourself.

At∑ Allotey (Ghana)   Thanks for your 'down-to-earth' approach and informative knowledge of Africa.

Augustine Mpofu (Zimbabwe)   Your sense of humour and ubiquitous behaviour kept 'Queen Bulabula' amused through difficult times.

Beatrice Howarth (Egypt)   For your warmth, support and wicked sense of humour, my soul sister!

Mrs E. Addy (Ghana)   My mother — the person who started it all, and who gave my the knowledge and love of diverse foods.

Eileen Haley (Spanish consultant)   The lynch pin between Mrs Marchanté and me. I promise to learn Spanish!

Mrs Emilia Marchanté (Cuba)   Dear Emilia, we deserve medals for wonderful cross-cultural communication: my negligible Spanish and your sparse English.

Felipe Lincy (Guadeloupe)   The elusive, comical French friend who kept my interest in Guadeloupe alive.

James and Nuala Hafner (my African–Australian Guinea Pigs)   My children: for your eternal patience and willingness to taste 'almost' everything I cooked! Thank you for believing in me and for all the typing and photocopying.

Dr Kwame Asumadu (Ghana)   My expert on Ashanti culture — for your generosity.

Lucia V. Rodrigues (Brazil)   For your speed in introducing me to Brazilian recipes, which have travelled half-way across the world.

Mike and Jenny Piper (Kenya)   Kenya will always be alive wherever you two go: 'Sukuma Wiki'.

Mrs Jigzie Campbell (Jamaica)   This is 'Fe we Africa/Jamaica connection — how we tek bad ting mek joke!'

Mrs Rita Pike and Ms Marlene Black (Jamaica)   Your wholesome Jamaica recipes have become family treasures.

Sofia Poppe (Tanzania)   The Tanzanian beauty with a magic touch in the kitchen. Thank you for your wonderful recipes and for always being there.

Cate Fowler (Australia)   Thank you for your encouragement and belief — many years ago.

Robyn Archer (Australia) and Ann Dunn (Australia)   Thank you for your continued support, advice and encouragement.

Ann-marie Mykyta (Australia)   For time and patience.

Julia de Roeper (Australia)   For supporting the project.

To all my friends — those too numerous to mention — whose combined presence and nurturing has been invaluable.

# FOREWORD

There is a famous saying that 'Africa always offers something new'.

Nowhere is this better expressed than in Dorinda Hafner's wonderful new book *A Taste of Africa*. In her selection of recipes and her recollections of the way of life and the foods of the countries she loves, Dorinda creates a portrait of Africa that is vital and interesting.

Whether she is telling a legend from a particular country, tracing the African influence on the food and culture of the Caribbean and the Americas or describing with great enthusiasm the delights of particular ingredients and recipes that are unusual to many western cooks, Dorinda captures the smells, the sounds and the tastes of Africa.

I recently made my first journey to South Africa — a very exciting, stimulating and moving experience. You don't have to go that far to be captivated by *A Taste of Africa*.

WHOOPI GOLDBERG

# INTRODUCTION

Although I am an African born and bred in Africa, I have lived on four continents and visited many countries around the world. Over the years I have seen and heard many Africans actively or passively denounce their roots in preference for totally different cultures. While travel and inter-cultural exchanges are healthy and should be encouraged, I remain immensely proud of my origins. For me, Africa continues to be as enigmatic and fascinating from within as from without.

*A Taste of Africa* is my modest contribution to the continent of my birth and to the stoic, quiet achievers who daily instil in the children of Africa the values of Africa's inherent wealth and a respect for a continent long designated as 'primitive' but which continues to shock and excite. What better way is there than with the double-edged sword of Africa's food: the variety, the diversity and quality of it in parts — and the lack of it in others.

Africa is making news world-wide, warts and all, with its colourful cultural splendours, its hunger, drought and politics. Africa is indeed enigmatic. The continent can boast some of the most exciting cuisine in the world and yet, paradoxically and tragically, some parts of it are starving. Perhaps by showing the world the positive picture of African cuisine I might in some small way highlight the plight of the starving millions on our continent and approach the problem from a different angle. 'The way to people's hearts is through their stomachs' is, in this context, a weird paradox indeed!

Parts of Africa, due to natural disasters, the fickleness of the elements, internecine conflicts and other extenuating circumstances, are experiencing phenomenal shortages of food crops, agricultural materials, water, and other necessities fundamental to sustaining life. But this does not mean that when and where these 'raw materials' are available Africa cannot boast of 'cuisines par excellence', easily standing alongside Asia, Europe and others of the world's best exponents of good food. The time has come to elucidate and elevate African cuisine to international status and to re-introduce both Africans and non-Africans alike to the intrinsic values of good, wholesome, cheap and yet tasty eating — the African way!

*A Taste of Africa* looks at food from ten different African countries, and from those countries across the Atlantic where African food has made itself at home since the iniquitous slave trading era. Among the African countries themselves, this book highlights both the similarity and diversity of preparation and cooking styles, such as the mixture of sweet and savoury in a main meal by the inclusion of fresh and dried fruits in North African cuisine, as opposed to the combination of meat, fish and vegetables in a single soup or stew as practised in countries south of the Sahara. Add to these continental differences the exciting changes which have transformed original African recipes into hybrid, culinary masterpieces by the integration of Portuguese, Spanish, French, Arawak and Carib Indian cooking traditions in places like South and Central America, the West Indies and Lousiana, and you begin to understand why I have chosen to write such a book. Investigating the similarities as well as the differences has been fascinating and exciting. I hope that this book will be both an invaluable addition to any personal cookbook collection and a useful guide on African food for academic and teaching institutions.

I had enormous difficulty in choosing the recipes because I wanted to pick those which, while easy to follow, made distinct statements about their African origins and at the same time showed the new cultural influences. Superficially this should have been easy, but some of my favourite recipes, once typed, sounded and looked unpalatable and my 'guinea pig' friends refused to try them!

Then there was the question of whether or not to include some of the more boring, although traditionally staple, African recipes, as well as the problem of major regional variations within the African continent itself. For example more fish is consumed in West Africa than meat; and more meat is consumed in East Africa than fish, generally because of the physical nature of the regions.

I also had to consider the problem of repetition since most of the ingredients are common to all the black cultures in question. Produce such as maize or corn, cassava, plantains, beans and okro (okra) are staple components of most black cuisine and appear in recipes that may appear quite similar yet also display regional and cultural variation. The continued inclusion of palm oil (dênde oil) in Latin, Central and North American cuisine as well as in the Caribbean, plus the similarity of methods of food preparation in dishes like Fufu (Foo-foo in Trinidad and Tabago), Caruru, Vatapa and Serapatel in Brazil, Moros y Cristianos con Platanos in Cuba, and Dirty Rice and Gumbo in Louisiana, only confirm the obvious cultural connections and also mark the distinct differences between Western dishes and cooking styles and the 'African' style of cooking.

Other differences between 'Western' and 'African' treatments of food are obvious when you realise that in parts of Africa quite heavy savoury meals are eaten for breakfast before departing for work in the mornings (foods such as Tom Brown or black-eyed beans with rice or gari) — a practice generally foreign to Westerners. Another major difference in eating habits is that meat is usually treated as a flavouring in African cooking and does not necessarily constitute the bulk of the main meal. I have only included a few recipes for sweets or desserts in this book to establish that they do exist as part of African cuisine, although among Africans south of the Sahara, desserts and sweets are not generally encouraged for traditional cultural reasons.

I have had enormous problems trying to translate my typically African 'let's estimate' style of cooking into easy-to-follow, easy-to-identify Western recipes. My mother and her mother before her have always cooked straight from their hearts and this is the way I, too, have learnt. I assumed it was going to be really easy to write for an audience to follow suit. What a rude awakening! In order to introduce traditional African cooking into modern kitchens, I have had to learn how to measure ingredients and give specific cooking temperatures and times — and that is the hardest thing of all for me. Many are the times at the butcher's that I have felt tempted to grab two chooks, one in each hand, to ascertain their comparative weights — the traditional way to determine how many people each bird would feed.

While I make no apologies for what I have written, I must be honest and tell you that I have tried as hard as I am able to give explanations for my 'modus operandi' and to measure most things for you, but I invite you to try to maintain the emotion and flow of the African cooking process. If you have never cooked intuitively before, here's your chance. Use common sense, your eyes and the feel of things to arrive at the correct amounts you need; but if you normally cook like this, then roll up your sleeves and go for it.

I hope you will have as much fun cooking and eating African food as I have had preparing it for, presenting it to, and sharing it with you. Bon appétit!

DORINDA HAFNER
June 1992

# GHANA

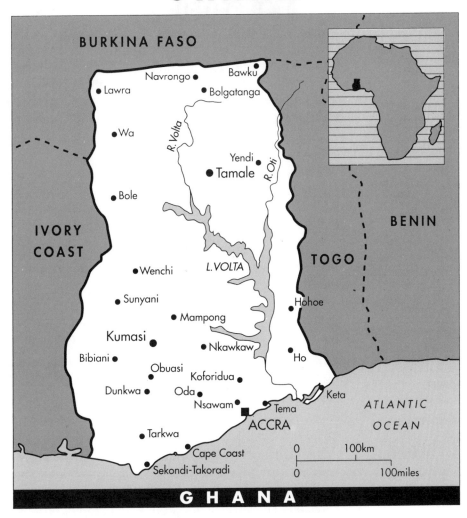

**Official title**   Republic of Ghana

**Capital city**   Accra

**Official language**   English, although Akan, Ewe, Ga and Dagbani are widely spoken

**Currency**   Cedi (C) = 100 pesewa

**Cash crops for export**   Cocoa, coffee, palm oil, copra, cola nuts, sheanut-butter and kenaf (the fibre is used like jute), limes

**Food crops**   Cassava, maize, millet, sorghum, rice, plantains, yams, poultry and domestic fish catch

**Total land area**   Approximately 240,000 sq km

# GROUNDNUT (PEANUT) SOUP WITH FOWL AND FUFU

1 kg (2 lb) lean meat e.g. chops, medallions of lamb shanks cut in chunks, or 6-8 pieces of jointed poultry or guinea fowl

Salt and pepper to taste

2 large onions, finely chopped

4 large, very ripe tomatoes or 400 g (13 oz) canned tomatoes

200 g (6½ oz) groundnut (peanut) paste or peanut butter

2 L (3½ pt) boiling water

Red chillies (hot peppers), fresh or ground, to taste (optional)

4-8 mushrooms (optional)

1 kg (2 lb) fish cutlets, salted, smoked, grilled, deep-fried or sundried

*Although the poultry traditionally used in this dish is guinea fowl, the meat of which is dark, chicken may of course be substituted. Remember that processed poultry will disintegrate quickly in the soup, so once it is cooked you should remove it from the pot until the soup has thickened. But do leave it long enough for the rich flavour of the creamy groundnut (peanut) and vegetable mixture to permeate the meat.*

*Groundnut (Peanut) Soup with Fowl is usually served with Fufu an Akan dumpling made from yams, cocoyams (taro), plantains, cassava or even processed potato flakes. The Fufu should sit like an island in a sea of soup, with the meat and fish scattered over the top. It is even referred to as the 'island in the sun'! This is a dish that is traditionally eaten with your fingers — even the soup!*

Put the meat or poultry in a very large, heavy-based saucepan (not a crockpot because the initial process of cooking requires fairly high heat and a crockpot does not provide enough heat to start with). Season meat with salt and pepper. Add the onions, stir together and cook 'dry' on medium heat, stirring continuously until the outside of the meat is slightly cooked and sealed.

Blanch the tomatoes in boiling water, peel off the skin and blend the flesh to a smooth juice. If using canned tomatoes, blend, then pour them into the meat and onion mixture and continue to simmer. Put the groundnut (peanut) paste or peanut butter into a big bowl, add 500 mL (¾ pt) of the boiling water and use a wooden spoon or a blender to blend the paste and water carefully together to form a creamy, smooth sauce.

Add this to the meat mixture with chillies (hot peppers) and mushrooms. Continue to simmer, stirring only occasionally to prevent the food sticking to the bottom of the pan. This is now the basic soup. Pour the rest of the boiling water into the soup and simmer slowly on medium heat to cook the meat for about

30–40 minutes, depending on the type of meat, used (guinea fowl takes longer).

Prepare your choice of fish by removing any residual bones. Add the fish either whole or in chunks to the soup towards the end of the cooking (during the last 30 minutes), to prevent it from breaking up in the soup. Once all the ingredients have been added, simmer slowly until the soup thickens.

SERVES 4

**900 mL (1½ pt) boiling water**

**90 g (3 oz) potato flour**

**200 mL (7 fl oz) cold water**

**1 packet (180 g/6 oz) potato flakes**

FUFU

Warm a medium saucepan with 200 mL (7 fl oz) of the boiling water. In a small jug blend the potato flour with 200 mL (7 fl oz) of lukewarm water (mixing some of the boiling water with part of the cold water; the water must not be hot or it will cook the starch) to form a creamy mixture.

Empty the water from the warmed saucepan. Pour the potato flakes into the saucepan and add the remaining boiling water, enough to fully cover the potato flakes. Do not stir yet.

Using a wooden spoon, stir the potato flour mixture in the jug and quickly add this to the saucepan. Speed is of the essence here, as is dexterity! Stir the 2 mixtures together vigorously, pulling the dough in from the centre against the inside of the saucepan with one hand and gripping the pan firmly with the other.

When the dough is firm and smooth, moisten a small bowl with small quantities of the cold water and scoop the dough into this bowl, either as one large ball or individual balls, and serve with soup.

SERVES 2

# DORINDA'S SPECIAL BAKED FISH

4 fresh medium fish e.g.
salmon, snapper, tuna or
trevally

40 g (1⅓ oz) root ginger,
finely grated

4 cloves garlic, finely
chopped

2 red chillies (hot
peppers), mashed into a
pulp

Salt to taste

10 g (2 teaspoons) butter

5 g (1 teaspoon) garlic
salt

170 g (5½ oz) canned crab
meat

4 cooked crayfish tails
(optional)

*This delicious seafood recipe should be served with homemade Chilli Sambal (pages 22–23) and plain Semolina or Cornmeal Dumplings (page 24). These combine three taste sensations: the delicate flavours of succulent fish, crayfish or crab; the bite of chilli, garlic and ginger; and the two are balanced and complemented by the dumplings. A typically coastal dish, it is another one usually eaten with your fingers! In Ghana we have a song called 'Komi ke loo', which is sung with this dish. 'Komi' (pronounced 'kormi') means corn (maize) dumpling; 'ke' (pronounced 'ker') means with; and 'loo' (pronounced 'low') means fish or meat.*

Scale and clean all the fish, remove the gills, and cut off the fins and the tails. Lie the fish flat on a chopping board and make 2 deep but short diagonal cuts in each side, leaving 1.5 cm (½ in) between the 2 cuts.

Prepare the seasoning by mixing the ginger, garlic, chillies (hot peppers) and salt into a paste and stuff some in the cuts on both sides. Rub the rest of the seasoning all over the fish.

Rub the butter over 4 pieces of aluminium foil. Place each fish on a piece of foil and sprinkle a pinch of garlic salt all over the fish. Loosely wrap up the foil to form parcels and bake for 30 minutes in an oven preheated to 180°C (350°F).

Wrap the crab meat in foil and warm in the oven for 10 minutes. Unwrap the baked fish and sprinkle the warm crab meat over each piece.

Serve each person with a piece of fish and a piece of crayfish tail, accompanied by a Chilli Sambal (pages 22–23) and the dumpling of your choice (page 24).

*Note:* You may choose to cook this dish without the seafood garnish, or to use fish cutlets instead of whole fish. If you use fish cutlets the seasoning remains the same but you just rub it all over the cutlets before baking, rather than inserting it into cuts. You need only bake cutlets for 20–25 minutes.

SERVES 4

# TRADITIONAL FRIED FISH
## KYENAM OR KENAN
### (TRADITIONAL NAMES PRONOUNCED 'CHINAM' OR 'KAYNANG')

**4 fresh medium fish e.g. salmon, snapper, tuna or trevally**

**45 g (1½ oz) root ginger, finely grated**

**2 red chillies (hot peppers), mashed into a pulp**

**Salt to taste**

**300 mL (½ pt) vegetable oil**

**Salt to taste**

*With so much of Ghana's fresh produce gathered from the ocean, I sometimes think that Ghanaians should have been born, with flippers and fins! Fish is eaten in all possible varieties and combinations in my country, so there is a lot of latitude to play with recipes and come up with your own favourites.*

Scale and clean all the fish, remove the gills, and cut off the fins and the tails. Lie the fish flat on a chopping board and make 2 deep but short diagonal cuts in each side, leaving 1.5 cm (½ in) between the 2 cuts.

Prepare the seasoning by mixing the ginger, chillies (hot peppers) and salt into a paste and stuff some in the cuts on both sides. Rub some of the remaining paste all over the fish.

Heat the oil in a skillet or deep frypan and deep-fry each fish until crisp and golden brown, being careful not to overcook. Remove the fish from the oil and drain. Serve hot, garnished with salad vegetables of your choice, such as lettuce, finely chopped spinach (silver beet), capsicums (sweet or bell peppers), tomatoes and onion.

*Note:* You may choose to grill your fish rather than deep-fry it.

SERVES 4

# KONTOMIRE NE MOMONE
## SPINACH WITH SMELLY SALTED FISH

1 medium dried, salted fish

4-8 whole baby plantains (apem), peeled

8 slices each cocoyam (taro) and yam (or 8 potatoes), peeled and diced

1 kg (2 lb) fresh spinach (silver beet), washed and chopped

2 small onions, finely chopped

4 tomatoes, finely diced

60 mL (4 tablespoons) vegetable oil

2 cloves garlic, finely chopped

15 g (1 tablespoon) turmeric

*Kontomire is the Ashanti word for the triangular leaves of the local cocoyam (taro) plant, which in Ghana and other parts of West Africa is called spinach. As kontomire may not be widely available, spinach (silver beet) can be substituted.*

*This recipe is a delicious specialty of the Ashanti and is often eaten for breakfast accompanied by one or a combination of baby plantains (apem), yams or cocoyams (taro). Contrary to its name, it is very tasty and wholesome!*

Soak the fish overnight to remove most of the salt. Rinse, clean and bone the fish. Shred into small pieces and set aside. Boil the plantains, cocoyams (taro), yams or potatoes in salted water until tender. Place the uncooked spinach (silver beet) inside a sieve and put that on top of the boiling vegetables to steam very lightly for about 5–7 minutes.

In Ghana we traditionally mash the spinach (silver beet), onions, tomatoes and half the fish in an apotoyiwa (pronounced 'apor-tor-ye-wa'), a round, earthenware bowl, with an eta (pronounced 'er-tah'), a flat-ended wooden masher, but in a modern kitchen I suggest you use an electric blender or food processor to blend these ingredients together.

Heat the oil in a small frypan, add the garlic and lightly fry until it begins to brown. Remove from the heat. Stir in the turmeric. (Traditionally palm oil is used in this recipe but vegetable oil mixed with turmeric makes a wonderful substitute).

Put the blended spinach (silver beet) mix in small individual bowl. Top each portion with 2 teaspoonfuls of the turmeric/garlic oil mix, and sprinkle with some of the leftover fish.

Decorate each bowl with boiled root vegetables and serve.

SERVES 4

**From Ghana**   Ghanaian Salad (page 21)

**From Ghana**    Dorinda's Special Baked Fish (page 14)

**From Ghana**    Cumin Roast Lamb (page 17)

# CUMIN ROAST LAMB

1 kg (2 lb) leg of lamb with most of the fat trimmed off

2 large sweet potatoes or yams, peeled or unpeeled

3 medium potatoes, peeled or unpeeled

MARINADE

60 g (4 tablespoons) ground cumin

15 g (1 tablespoon) garlic salt

75 mL (5 tablespoons) polyunsaturated oil

GRAVY

Boiling water

10 g (2 teaspoons) cornflour (cornstarch) mixed with 30 mL (2 tablespoons) cold water

*When I go to the butcher's to buy a leg of lamb for this recipe, I'm frequently tempted to revert to the 'home' method of selecting which one to buy. At home in Ghana I would hold a leg in each hand and jiggle them up and down to work out which had enough meat to feed the family. These days, to avoid embarrassing my children, I can only resort to pointing gamely at the one I think will be enough to feed us — such is progress.*

Thoroughly rinse the leg of lamb under the cold tap and dry it with paper towels. Lay the lamb in a roasting pan. Make 3–4 deep cuts in each side of the lamb.

To make the marinade, combine all ingredients in a small bowl and mix well. Insert in the cuts and spoon the rest all over the leg of lamb.

Cover with aluminium foil and stand for at least 2 hours. The longer the meat stands, the stronger the flavour will be. Bake for 30 minutes in an oven preheated to 220°C (425°F) then lower the heat and bake at 180°C (350°F) for another hour or until the meat is tender and cooked.

Wash and cut each sweet potato into 3 portions and each ordinary potato into 2 portions. Lay the ordinary potatoes flat on their backs with the white sides uppermost and sprinkle with salt to help brown them. Arrange sweet and ordinary potatoes beside the meat in the last hour of cooking.

When the meat is cooked, slice and serve it with the potatoes, gravy, steamed spinach (silver beet) and corn.

To make the gravy, add boiling water to the bottom of the roasting pan with the cornflour (cornstarch) mixture.

*Note:* You may choose to do what I sometimes do by stuffing all the potatoes with the steamed spinach (silver beet) and corn (maize) kernels before serving

SERVES 4–6

# THE LEGEND OF THE GOLDEN STOOL

The Ashanti are part of a larger group of Akan-speaking peoples. Centuries ago wars periodically broke out between the different kingdoms of these people and the custom was for the loser to send a member of the royal household to serve the victor in his kingdom.

The kingdom of Denkyira annexed the budding Ashanti kingdom and the Ashanti prince, Osei-Tutu, was sent to wait upon the Denkyiran king Nana Boa Amponsem. In Denkyira Osei-Tutu was befriended by a fetish priest Okomfo Anokye who had come from the kingdom of Akwamu.

As the Ashanti was, and still is, a matriarchal society, when the king of the Ashanti died, Osei-Tutu, his maternal nephew, was called home to assume the throne. He asked to be allowed to take Okomfo Anokye with him. In time Okomfo Anokye became the most influential high priest of the Ashanti, giving spiritual protection to the kingdom.

To cement his friendship with King Osei-Tutu, Okomfo Anokye decided to conjure from the heavens a solid gold stool with the power to make the Ashanti invincible.

As part of the eight-day ritual he took two saplings of a native 'kum' tree and planted them some distance apart, proclaiming that whichever lived would mark the site of the new capital of the kingdom.

He then took the 'akonfena', the sword of state, and marked a spot where a hole was to be dug in which he would be buried. While entombed he would consult the tribal elders who had preceded him and would be given supernatural powers to pass on to the Ashanti.

He charged everyone not to cry if he did not return within eight days for, he explained, he could only return if no tears were shed. Before his burial he promised that on the third day the golden stool would descend from heaven.

Legend has it that this is exactly what happened, but tragically, when Okomfo Anokye had not reappeared by the eighth day, the Ashanti women began to wail and he was lost forever.

The sapling that lived marked the capital of the new kingdom which was called Kumasi (meaning under 'kum'), and which is still the capital of the Ashanti today. The place where the other sapling died marks the present-day town of Kumawu. The sword of state remains to this day inextricable from the ground into which Okomfo Anokye thrust it, and the golden stool, the symbol of the power of the Ashanti, many believe rests at the Ashanti place.

# PALAVA SAUCE

250 mL (8 fl oz) palm oil

4 medium onions, finely chopped

4 large tomatoes, blanched, peeled and mashed

Salt and pepper to taste

2-4 red chillies (hot peppers), finely chopped (optional)

250 g (½ lb) diced cooked meat or leftovers (optional, although not chicken) and/or 250 g (½ lb) fish e.g. snapper, tuna, salmon or trevally

125 g (¼ lb) smoked herring, boned (optional)

200 g (6½ oz) dried prawns (shrimp)

3 bunches of spinach (silver beet) or 750 g (1½ lb) frozen spinach (silver beet), washed and chopped

100 g (3½ oz) egushi (shelled pumpkin seeds or pepitas), ground in a coffee grinder

*There are many variations of this traditional spinach (silver beet) dish from West Africa. No-one can agree to its origins — some say it is Nigerian, others claim it comes from Ghana, but my mother says her version comes from Sierra Leone!*

*In West Africa 'palava' means business or trouble, so I suppose this dish can also be called, literally, Trouble Sauce. Actually it is a stew rather than a sauce, a rich blend of spinach (silver beet), egushi (pumpkin seeds), prawns (shrimp), meat and smoked herring or snapper. Despite its name, it is no trouble to cook and certainly no trouble to eat!*

Heat the oil in a saucepan and fry the onions until golden. Add the tomatoes, pepper to taste and the chillies (hot peppers).

If you are using corn oil (see Note) add turmeric here. Cook for 10–15 minutes on low heat, stirring regularly (not continuously).

Add salt to taste with your choice of diced, cooked meat and fish. Stir in the smoked herring with the dried prawns (shrimp). Simmer on very low heat, stirring regularly to prevent burning.

Add the spinach (silver beet) to the meat mixture. Cover and simmer on low heat for 10–15 minutes or until the spinach (silver beet) is soft and cooked. Stir regularly, taking care not to break up the fish too much.

Add the egushi (pumpkin seeds) and stir them into the sauce. Cook for a further 10–15 minutes on low heat.

Serve hot with boiled rice, yams, plantains, gari (coarse cassava flour), Banku (cornmeal dumplings) or any root vegetable, roasted, boiled or grilled.

*Note:* Palmoil is red oil from the red, tropical, palm kernel. It is used for making a variety of foods, such as some digestive biscuits. You can substitute corn oil and 4 teaspoons of turmeric to give a similar visual and culinary effect.

SERVES 4

# OKRO STEW

400 g (13 oz) okro (okra)

300 mL (½ pt) oil, preferably palm oil (see Note)

3-4 medium onions, finely chopped

2 medium eggplants (aubergines), peeled and finely diced

50 g (1½ oz) root ginger, grated

1-4 red chillies (hot peppers), finely chopped (optional)

4 large, ripe tomatoes, blanched, peeled and mashed or 200 g (6½ oz) canned tomatoes, mashed

150 g (5 oz) dried prawns (shrimp)

30 g (1 oz) piece of salted dried fish of your choice e.g. herring, shredded

150 g (5 oz) diced smoked ham and/or 4 small pieces of boiled pigs' trotters (you can substitute some other meat or more fish, crab or yabbies, but not chicken)

OPTIONAL EXTRAS
Pinch of ground 'kaawé' or traditional stone, thought to enhance the 'tackiness' of the okro (okra)

Small piece of cured, salted beef

*It has only been every so often in my life that I have come across a dish that seems to surfeit all my senses! Okro Stew is one. With its clever mix of seafood, smoked ham, dried salted fish, and vegetables such as okra (okro, as it is called in Africa), eggplant (aubergine), tomatoes and onions, it smells good, tastes sensational and even feels good, with a wonderful smooth texture. I always feel that this is the food that can win wars!*

Trim off the ends of the okro (okra) and slice it into thin rounds about 1.5 cm (½ in) in diameter. In a large, heavy saucepan, heat the oil and fry the onions until they are light brown. Stirring all the time, add the sliced okro (okra), eggplants (aubergines), 'kaawé', ginger, chillies (hot peppers) and mashed tomato in that order but allow 3 minutes simmering time between each addition. This dish burns easily so stir regularly.

Simmer for about 10 minutes on low heat. Add the dried prawns (shrimp), salted dried fish, salted beef, smoked ham, pigs' trotters and any other, meat, fish or crustacean. Simmer for a further 10–15 minutes until all ingredients are blended in and cooked, not 'mushy'.

Serve hot with a variety of carbohydrates, such as boiled rice, 'Banku' (cornmeal dumplings), boiled potatoes, yams, cocoyams, (taro), plantains (giant, tropical bananas), cassava, gari (coarse cassava powder).

Note: If using plain vegetable oil, add 10 g (2 teaspoons) of turmeric.

SERVES 4

# GHANAIAN SALAD

2 large Spanish onions, sliced in very thin rings

Wine or cider vinegar for marinating

1 medium cucumber

1 lettuce, washed whole

440 g (14 oz) canned baked beans in tomato sauce

425 g (13½ oz) canned red salmon or other fish, drained

400 g (12 oz) canned sweet corn, drained

250 mL (8 fl oz) mayonnaise

125 mL (4 fl oz) soya milk

150 g (5 oz) snow peas (mange tout), washed, topped and tailed

4 firm, ripe tomatoes, sliced in rings

sliced avocado pears (optional)

4 potatoes or sweet potatoes (yams), boiled then diced

3 hard-boiled eggs, sliced in rounds

*The kaleidoscope of colours brought to this dish by the wonderful variety of ingredients only hints at its exciting combination of textures and flavours. With eggs and fish and a wide range of fresh vegetables, the Ghanaian Salad is delicious and healthy and a meal on its own served with warm herbed bread and chilled water garnished with watercress or basil.*

Marinate the onions in wine or cider vinegar for 30 minutes. Deeply score the cucumber vertically with a fork along the sides from top to bottom, then slice thinly into rounds. Cut the lettuce in half vertically then into thin half-moon strips. Place the baked beans in tomato sauce in one bowl and the red salmon in another bowl (you can use a variety of fish for more flavour). Put the sweet corn into a third bowl. Blend the mayonnaise with the soya milk to use as dressing.

Using a huge, preferably deep and oval-shaped salad dish, arrange alternate layers of the ingredient and dressing. Continue until you finish almost everything. Leave some egg, snow peas (mange tout) and dressing for the final topping to finish it aesthetically. Store in the refrigerator for at least 1 hour before serving. This salad can also be made the day before if it is refrigerated. When ready to serve, slice it like a cake, lift out and serve with your favourite bread.

SERVES 8

# SHITOR DIN

TRADITIONAL DARK CHILLI SAMBAL

350 mL (12 fl oz) vegetable oil

4 medium onions, finely chopped

100 g (3½ oz) root ginger, finely grated

30 g (2 tablespoons) tomato paste

2 chicken stock cubes

200 g (6½ oz) peeled dried prawns (shrimp)

100 g (3½ oz) tiny prawns (shrimp), ground to a powder

75 g (2½ oz) chilli (hot pepper) powder

*Many African recipes combine filling, although rather bland, dishes made from grains or vegetables with spicy sauces, soups and condiments to provide the flavour. Chilli Sambal is one of these zesty additions and can be used to pep up not only grain or vegetable-based dishes, but seafood, poultry and meat recipes, too. Here are three Chilli Sambal recipes known collectively as 'Shitor'. Two are traditional: the one made from fresh ingredients will keep for only a day or two. The other two can be kept in the refrigerator for up to a year.*

Heat the oil in a heavy-based saucepan and fry the onions and ginger for 10–15 minutes until the onions are golden. Stir in the tomato paste and mix thoroughly.

Crush the chicken stock cubes and add them to the pan, without water. Stir to mix. Simmer, stirring frequently, for 3 minutes. Add both lots of prawns (shrimp) and stir for 1 minute. Add the chilli (hot pepper) powder and thoroughly blend in. Cook for 2 more minutes, stirring continuously. Be careful not to burn the mixture at this stage. Remove from the heat and stand for about 1 hour or until the sambal has cooled down. Transfer to a storage jar and keep in a cool place until required.

MAKES APPROXIMATELY 750 g (1½ lb)

6 fresh red chillies (hot peppers), finely chopped

1 medium onion, finely chopped

3 large tomatoes, blanched, peeled and chopped

Salt to taste

## FRESH SHITOR

Combine chillies (hot peppers), onion and tomatoes in a bowl and mash or process to a pulp. Season and serve as a side dish or sauce.

MAKES 2 SERVINGS

350 mL (12 fl oz) vegetable oil

8 cloves garlic, finely chopped

4 medium onions, finely chopped

100 g (3½ oz) root ginger, coarsely grated (with or without skin)

30 g (2 tablespoons) tomato paste

2 chicken stock cubes

150 g (5 oz) dried prawns (shrimp)

100 g (3½ oz) dried, tiny prawns (shrimp)

100 g (3½ oz) chilli (hot pepper) powder

## DORINDA'S SHITOR DIN OR MAKO TUNTUM

Heat the oil in a heavy-based saucepan and fry the garlic, onions and ginger for 10–15 minutes until the onions are golden. Stir in the tomato paste and mix thoroughly.

Crush the chicken stock cubes and add that to the pan, without water. Add both lots of dried prawns (shrimp) and stir for 1 minute. Add the chilli (hot pepper) powder and thoroughly mix in.

Remove from the heat and stand for about 1 hour or until the sambal has cooled down. Transfer to a storage jar and keep in a cool place until required.

*Note:* This sambal can be stored for up to 1 year in the refrigerator, so you can make a large quantity and freeze in several small containers.

MAKES APPROXIMATELY 750 g (1½ lb)

# DUMPLINGS

**Salt to taste**

**1.5 L (2½ pt) water**

**600 g (1¼ lb) fermented corn (maize) dough If corndough is unavailable make Semolina Dumplings, below**

BANKU (CORNMEAL DUMPLINGS)

*Grains are the staple produce throughout the African continent and are used extensively in African cuisine. Sadly, in some areas there is little other produce available. Corn (maize) is frequently used to make dumplings, which are used in many kinds of dishes, from soups to meat and poultry.*

Salt the water and bring to a boil in a very heavy-based saucepan or cast iron pot. Reserve half the boiling water and keep at a slow boil.

Add the corn (maize) dough to the rest of the water in the pot. Stir vigorously with a wooden spoon, press against the inside of the pot to eliminate lumps as the dumpling cooks. Continue to press the dough against the insides of the pot, adding small quantities of the reserved boiling water until the dough tastes less floury, softens and cooks through.

Remove from the pot, form into balls the size of tennis balls and serve with the sauces of your choice.

SERVES 4

**Salt to taste**

**750 mL (1¼ pt) water**

**500 g (1 lb) semolina**

SEMOLINA DUMPLINGS

Salt the water and bring to a boil in a very heavy-based saucepan or cast iron pot. Reserve half the boiling water and keep at a slow boil.

Add the semolina to the rest of the water in the pot. Stir vigorously with a wooden spoon and press against the inside of the pot to eliminate lumps as the dumpling cooks.

Keep adding small amounts of the reserved boiling water to make the dumpling soft and easier to knead. Continue to press the dough against the insides of the pot until it tastes less 'gritty', softens and cooks.

Remove from the pot, form into balls the size of tennis balls and serve with the sauces of your choice.

SERVES 2–4

# TOM BROWN

TOASTED CORNMEAL PORRIDGE

**90 g (3 oz) ablémamu (finely ground, roasted corn or maize)**

**150 mL (¼ pt) hot milk**

**10 g (2 teaspoons) brown sugar or 30 mL (1 oz) sweet condensed milk combined with 125 mL (4 fl oz) very hot water**

*Many West African school children call this dish 'Tom Brown'; others call it 'Laying Concrete'! The name was coined from Tom Brown's School Days because the recipe is so often served at boarding school.*

*When made properly (as opposed to the lumpish mass I remember being dished up at school) it is absolutely delicious and quite addictive!*

*To make the ablémamu (ground corn or maize), use ordinary popcorn, but dry roast it rather than cooking it in oil. Remove it from the heat just before it begins to pop, then cool and grind it finely in a coffee grinder. Cool again overnight and store in an airtight container. It's always better to use freshly roasted and ground corn (maize) for the smell alone!*

Place the corn powder in a medium cereal bowl. Pour in the hot milk and add the sugar. Stir to mix thoroughly. It thickens and swells to form a typical Tom Brown porridge. Sit back, smell it, tuck in and … enjoy.

SERVES 1

---

## THE FIRST INDEPENDENT AFRICAN NATION

The name Ghana originated under a prosperous and longstanding Sudanese empire that formed part of the pre-European network of trade routes linking the Guinea Coast (West Africa) to North Africa across the Sahara.

After European colonisation, Ghana was made up of the former colonies of the Gold Coast, the lands of the Ashanti people and the Trust Territory of Togoland (now the Republic of Togo). As a consequence, Ghana shares traditions and beliefs, culture and foods with parts of neighbouring Togo, Ivory Coast and Nigeria.

The present Republic of Ghana came into existence in 1957 when the country became the first African nation to gain independence south of the Sahara.

# KUBÉCAKE

500 g (1 lb) desiccated or finely grated, fresh coconut

200 g (6½ oz) root ginger, grated (or less to taste)

Dark rum (approx. 200 mL (6½ fl oz) or according to taste)

315 g (10 oz) cane or caster sugar

*Kubécake is a sweet sold by street hawkers throughout West Africa. It is not actually a cake as its name suggests; rather it is an explosion of two fiery forces, a combination of strong, dark rum and ginger, with the balancing sweetness of sugar. In fact, Kubécake is a version of what Europeans commonly call rum balls.*

In a bowl, mix the coconut and ginger with a generous amount of rum. Keep it warm in a preheated but not hot oven.

Melt the sugar in a heavy-based saucepan on medium to low heat. When the sugar starts to go brown at the edges stir with a wooden spoon until smooth.

When the sugar is brown (not light brown, and not dark brown but brown), quickly add the coconut/rum mixture. The timing here is critical. The mixture may bubble but ignore that and stir vigorously until the sugar is well blended with all the ingredients. Remove from the heat and cool for about 30 minutes.

Form into small balls about the size of a table tennis ball. Serve immediately or refrigerate and serve later.

*Note:* The trickiest part in making this recipe is the timing of the sugar temperature during browning, so stay close and keep a critical eye on the process.

SERVES 4–10 (depending on sweet tooths!)

# IVORY COAST

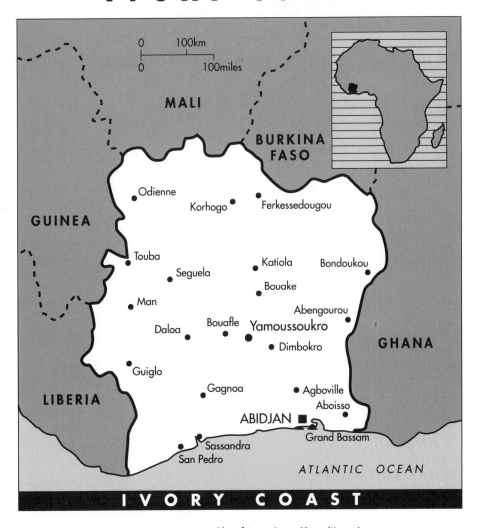

**Official title**  Republic of Ivory Coast (Cote d'Ivoire)

**Capital city**  Yamoussoukro is the political capital, while Abidjan is the economic centre

**Official language**  French

**Currency**  CFA franc = 100 centimes

**Cash crops for export**  Cocoa, coffee, sugar, bananas, pineapples, cotton, rubber, coconut palm, palm oil and vegetable oil

**Food crops**  Rice, maize, millet, sorghum, cassava, yams, plantains and sweet potatoes

**Total land area**  Approximately 323,000 sq km

# PALMNUT SOUP WITH FUFU

125 mL (4 oz) water

1 kg (2 lb) lean lamb shanks or chops, or shoulder of beef cut in chunks

Salted pigs' trotters, jointed and cleaned

Salt and pepper to taste

2 large onions, finely chopped

3 large, ripe tomatoes, blanched, peeled and puréed

750 g (1½ lb) palmnut pulp

250 mL (8 fl oz) boiling water

Chilli pepper or fresh, ground red chillies (hot peppers) to taste, (optional)

4 large mushrooms, cleaned and peeled

2 giant crabs cooked whole in salted water and drained (remove legs but not the claws – save cooked legs to be added separately to the soup)

1 kg (2 lb) fish cutlets (salted, smoked, grilled, deep-fried or sundried)

*Crab meat forms just one of the ingredients of this filling soup based on the pulp of palmnuts. Traditionally, the pulp is extracted by pounding the fleshy exterior of the palmnut, but for the Western kitchen tinned palmnut pulp has to suffice. Luckily it tastes just as good as the fresh and is available in most capital cities of the world. The palm from which the nuts are gathered grows in many tropical areas, from West Africa to Malaysia, New Guinea, Fiji and Brazil. Palmnut Soup is another dish that traditionally is eaten with Fufu (page 13). This combination dish is common to West Africa.*

Place the water, the meat and the pigs' trotters in a very large, heavy-based saucepan (not a crockpot because the initial process of cooking this dish requires fairly high heat and a crockpot does not afford that level of heat to start with). Season to taste with salt and pepper. Stir in the onions and cook 'dry' on medium heat, stirring continuously, until the outside of the meat is 'sealed'. Add the tomatoes. Continue to simmer for 10–15 minutes.

In a large bowl, combine the palmnut pulp with the boiling water, beating with a wooden spoon to form a creamy, smooth consistency. Add this to the meat mixture with ground chillies (hot peppers), the mushrooms, giant crabs and crab legs. Simmer on medium heat for 30–40 minutes, stirring only occasionally to prevent food sticking to the bottom of the pan.

Prepare your choice of smoked, grilled, deep-fried or sundried fish by removing any residual bones. Add the fish either whole or in chunks to the soup during the last 30 minutes to prevent it from breaking up too much and becoming 'mushy' in the soup. Once all the ingredients are added, continue to simmer slowly until soup thickens.

Serve hot with Fufu. You may choose to continue simmering the soup to thicken it and turn it into a palmnut stew, in which case you serve it with gari (page 30) or cassava powder, rice or the carbohydrate of your choice.

SERVES 4–6

# GIANT CRAB THERMIDOR

**60 mL (4 tablespoons) vegetable oil**

**3 shallots (spring onions) cleaned and finely chopped**

**1 large green capsicum (sweet or bell pepper), finely chopped**

**15 g (1 tablespoon) grated root ginger**

**6 cloves garlic, finely chopped**

**2 red chillies (hot peppers), finely chopped**

**1 fresh tomato, finely chopped**

**15 g (1 tablespoon) tomato paste**

**60 g (2 oz) dried prawns (shrimp), blended in a coffee grinder to a powder**

**750 g (1½ lb) cooked crab meat**

**Salt and pepper to taste**

**8-12 empty crab shells (request these from your fishmonger)**

**125 g (4 oz) ablémamu (for roasted, ground corn powder, see introduction to Tom Brown on page 25)**

**Sprigs of fresh coriander (cilantro)**

**Black pepper**

*When crabs are in season, the ones caught on the Ivory Coast always seem to be the biggest! This is my interpretation of a delicious Ivorian equivalent to Lobster Thermidor.*

*My first experience of how painful a bite from a crab can be was when I was ten years old and helping my grandmother to prepare this dish. She had a seaside kitchen from which it was easy to gather the live crabs that had been caught in the traditional woven baskets known as ' flotor'. Luckily, it is now possible to buy cooked crab meat from supermarkets and fishmongers and so avoid the nips!*

In a pan, heat the oil and sauté the shallots (spring onions), capsicum (sweet or bell pepper), ginger, garlic, chillies (hot peppers), and tomato for about 10 minutes, stirring constantly. Add the tomato paste and the prawn (shrimp) powder. Mix well and cook on low heat for 5 minutes. Add the crab meat and stir in well. Taste the mixture and, if necessary, add salt and pepper. Be careful, as prawn (shrimp) powder can be very salty.

Fill each crab shell with some of the mixture, then sprinkle the top of each full shell with the ablémamu. Bake for 3–4 minutes in an oven preheated to 220°C (425°F) until the tops brown a little, being careful not to burn them. Serve hot, straight out of the oven, garnished with fresh coriander (cilantro) and a dash of black pepper.

SERVES 4–6

# CASSAVA

Cassava is a staple part of the diet of many African nations, as well as in Brazil, the West Indies and other countries to which the African people have spread.

Cassava is grown for its edible tuberous roots, which provide a nutritious starch. It may be cooked whole or pounded to pulp for use in a variety of dishes, but one of the most widespread and productive forms of cassava is as a granular powder of varying consistency. Most popular when it is coarsely ground, this powder is known as gari in West Africa, farinhe de mandioca (manioc is another name for cassava) in Portugese-speaking black areas, and farine de manioc in French-speaking black areas. Cassava powder is better known in Western countries as tapioca.

Whether it is known as gari or farinhe de mandioca, cassava powder is a superb and nutritious thickening agent for soups and stews, and the granules may also be prepared to eat as an accompaniment to other dishes, and can take the place of rice or couscous.

COOKING GARI

To prepare gari or farinhe de mandioca for use as an accompaniment put 150 g (5 oz) gari in a bowl and add enough lightly salted cold water to cover it completely. Allow it to stand for 10 minutes until the gari absorbs the liquid and swells (like rice, gari will swell to about twice its original size). Fluff out the gari with a fork and serve with a hot dish, preferably with a sauce.

# ATSIEKE

**500 g (1 lb) smoked herring, mackeral or snapper, scaled and cleaned**

**Salt to taste**

**15 g (3 teaspoons) finely grated ginger**

**125 mL (4 fl oz) vegetable or groundnut (peanut) oil**

**2 onions, finely chopped**

**4 ripe tomatoes, blanched, peeled and puréed**

**15 g (1 tablespoon) tomato paste blended with 60 mL (4 tablespoons) water**

**2 red chillies (hot peppers) finely chopped**

**250 g (8 oz) green beans, chopped**

**Garlic salt to taste**

**150 g (5 oz) gari (coarse cassava powder)**

*Pronounced 'acherker', Atsieke is 'street' food at its best. Particularly popular at the street stalls and roadside cafes of the colourful Abidjan (the country's economic centre) suburb of Treichville, Atsieke is made from gari (coarse cassava powder) and served with fish and Chilli Sambal (page 22) or Pepper Sauce (page 101). It can also be served with a combination meat and vegetable sauce.*

Season the fish with salt and ginger. Heat the oil in a heavy-based pan and sauté the fish until crisp and brown. Remove from the oil, drain, set aside and keep hot.

In the remaining hot oil, add the onions and sauté till almost brown, then add the tomatoes, tomato paste, chillies (hot peppers), green beans, garlic salt, meat (if used) and any other chopped vegetables of your choice. Cover and simmer for 10–15 minutes or until the meat is tender.

Put the gari (coarse cassava powder) in a bowl and add enough lightly salted cold water to just cover it completely. Allow it to stand for 10 minutes until gari (coarse cassava powder) absorbs the liquid and swells. Fluff out the gari (coarse cassava powder) with a fork and serve with the sauce and a piece of fried fish each.

SERVES 4

# KEJENOU

**4 chicken portions cleaned and jointed**

**6 large green prawns (shrimp), peeled and deveined**

**10 g (2 teaspoons) each garlic salt and paprika, mixed together**

**250 mL (8 fl oz) groundnut (peanut) oil**

**2 onions, finely chopped**

**4 cloves garlic, finely chopped**

**4 ripe tomatoes, blanched, peeled and puréed**

**15 mL (1 tablespoon) tomato paste blended with 125 mL (4 fl oz) water**

**2 red chillies (hot peppers), finely chopped**

**5 g (1 teaspoon) each ground cinnamon, nutmeg and saffron powder**

**400 g (13 oz) long-grain white rice**

**1-1.5 L (1¾-2½ pt) chicken stock or equal quantities sweet white wine and stock**

**Parsley to garnish**

**Small cube of butter**

**1 whole lettuce**

*This is a treasured Ivorian dish, invariably made with chicken and vegetables cooked together, traditionally, in an earthenware pot. Pronounced 'kay-jay-nu', it is a 'special occasion' recipe.*

Season the chicken and prawns (shrimp) with garlic salt and paprika and leave for 2–4 hours. In a frying pan, heat the oil and sauté the chicken and prawns (shrimp). Remove the prawns (shrimp) when they turn 'pink' and the chicken when it is cooked and brown. Set both aside.

Add the onions and garlic to the same oil and sauté until the onions start to brown, then stir in the tomatoes, tomato paste, chillies (hot peppers), cinnamon, nutmeg and saffron. Simmer for 5 minutes then add the chicken, rice and half the chicken stock. Taste and adjust the seasoning. Divide the mixture into four individual ramekins.

Cover each one and simmer slowly on low heat, stirring periodically to avoid sticking or burning. Divide the rest of the stock between the ramekins in small amounts as necessary until the rice and meat are cooked and moist. This dish is not meant to be very dry. When cooked, garnish each individual portion with parsley and a small amount of the butter and the reserved prawns (shrimp). Serve hot with a lettuce leaf covering each dish.

*Note:* This dish is best cooked and served in individual portions.

SERVES 4

**From Ghana** Palava Sauce (page 19) with boiled plantain

**From Ghana** Okro Stew (page 20)

**From Ivory Coast and Ghana**   Palmnut Soup (page 28) with Fufu (Dumpling) (Page 13)

**From Ivory Coast** Baked Plantain Loaf (page 35), grilled pieces of plantain, and peanuts, with watermelon juice

# COLD GUINEA FOWL

1 whole, large guinea fowl

Salt to taste

6 whole garlic cloves

15 mL (1 tablespoon) each fresh orange juice and lemon or lime juice

500 mL (¾ pt) sweet apple cider

10 g (2 teaspoons) freshly ground black pepper

15 mL (1 tablespoon) vegetable oil

Dash orange essence combined with a dash orange oil (found in health food shops)

*In some areas of Africa guinea fowl are more common than chickens. Frequently they are free-range birds and their meat is darker and tastes stronger than that of chicken. This is a particularly tangy and aromatic recipe due to the blend of citrus juices and cider, and is perfect to serve with a green salad on a hot day.*

Season the guinea fowl inside and out with the salt and garlic cloves, leaving some cloves inside the fowl and some embedded in the skin. Combine the fruit juices, sweet cider and pepper, and pour over the fowl in a saucepan.

Cover and simmer gently for 1½–2 hours, turning over from time to time. You may need to add more cider or some chicken stock to prevent burning and to ensure there is enough fluid to fully cook the fowl.

When cooked, remove the fowl from the juices and brush all over with the vegetable oil mixed with orange essence and oil and brown the fowl quickly in an oven preheated to 230°C (450°F). When brown, remove and cool. Joint the fowl before serving with a green salad garnished with pineapple and orange slices.

SERVES 4–6

## GUINEA FOWLS

Guinea fowls are the most commonly eaten form of poultry in several African countries. Store-bought processed chickens are beyond the price range of many people. Guinea fowls are often caught from the wild, raised in the backyard or sold door-to-door by hawkers. The meat of guinea fowls is stronger and darker than chicken, and the yolks of guinea fowl eggs are richer and yellower. Such eggs are considered a delicacy and are often sold boiled at street stalls.

One of the funniest images I have of Africa is the commotion as an entire household, young and old alike, chases an escaped fowl round and round the backyard with assorted native implements in hand to do the bird in!

# RICE AND OFFAL BALLS

500 g (1 lb) minced cooked liver, offal or leftover meat

1 onion, finely chopped

250 g (½ lb) boiled rice

1 egg

5 g (1 teaspoon) garlic powder or 3 cloves garlic, finely chopped

5 g (1 teaspoon) garlic salt

1 teaspoon (5 g) freshly ground white pepper

Wholemeal breadcrumbs

2 eggs, beaten with 15 mL (1 tablespoon) milk

250 mL (8 oz) vegetable oil for deep-frying

*I realise there are some people who can't face the thought of eating any kind of offal, so it is just as permissible to use up offcuts of meat in this recipe. Personally I think liver and the like is delicious and this particular dish is not only tasty, nutritious and inexpensive, but also a very efficient means of dressing mutton up as lamb — if you will pardon the pun!*

In a bowl, combine the meat, onion, rice, egg, garlic powder or chopped garlic, garlic salt and pepper. Mix well to form a firm dough.

Form into small balls (the size of table tennis balls). Roll each ball in the breadcrumbs and then the egg and milk mix. Heat the oil in a frying pan and, when hot, fry the balls until cooked inside and golden on the outside (check the first one cooked). Drain and serve with fresh greens as a snack.

SERVES 4

## THE LEGEND OF THE CRABS

Back in the days when old people's hair didn't turn grey, an orphan called Afua (which means a girl born on Friday) was sent to live with her aunt and uncle. The old couple did not want her, so they would not tell her their names, but refused to give her any protein to eat until she could discover them. Afua was also made to perform many household tasks, one of which was to fill a huge drum with water.

Afua would take the drum to the river and weep because she had no way of guessing their names. Several crabs lived in the riverbed, protected by clay because in those days crabs had no shells. They heard Afua's distress and decided to help her for they knew that the old couple would walk by the river.

One night the crabs heard the couple call each other by name. The next morning when Afua arrived to fill the drum they excitedly told her. When Afua returned to her aunt and uncle she was able to call them by their names.

The couple was furious and realised that it must have been the crabs who had divulged their secret. In a rage they took some shell-shaped gourds (calabashes) and flung them at the crabs so hard that they lodged on the crabs' backs. In retaliation the crabs threw grey clay back at the old pair, which stuck in their hair.

This is why crabs now have shells — and why old people go grey, a reminder to the world that older people should be wiser and kinder.

# BAKED PLANTAIN LOAF

**3 large, very ripe plantains**

**2 teaspoons (10 g) fresh shitor din (chilli sambal, page 23)**

**250 g (8 oz) rice flour**

**Salt to taste**

**60 mL (2 fl oz) corn oil**

**2 teaspoons (10 g) turmeric powder**

Peel the plantains, cut them into small chunks and put into a large, deep mixing bowl. Mash into a thick paste with your fingers or an electric blender. If using a blender, you may need to add 30—60 mL (1—2 fl oz) of water for smoother blending.

Add the shitor din, rice flour and salt and mix well. Gently heat the corn oil in a frypan and add the turmeric. Stir well, remove from the heat and blend into the plantain mixture which should be thick yet soft enough to pour. If it is too soft, add small amounts of rice flour (a teaspoonful at a time) or if too stiff, add small amounts of water until it reaches the described consistency.

Grease a loaf tin, and pour plantain mixture into it. Bake in the oven on medium to low heat at 150—180°C (300—350°F) for 1 hour or until cooked and firm.

When cooked, remove from the oven and allow to stand for approximately 5—10 minutes before turning it out on to a wire rack. Slice and serve with salted groundnuts (peanuts), or as an accompaniment to dishes as you wish.

SERVES 4

# MANGO FOOL

**20 very ripe mangoes, washed and peeled**

**60 mL (4 tablespoons) Cointreau (optional)**

**500 mL (¾ pt) thick cream (optional)**

**Fresh mint sprigs, glacé or fresh fruit to decorate**

*Traditionally, puddings are not eaten in Africa; when they are it is part of the Western culture that since colonisation has been grafted over the tradition. What is more common is to finish a meal with fruit, and to my mind mangoes are one of the best there is! There are many different varieties of mango in Africa and during the mango season the fruit becomes so plentiful it is hard to know what to do with it all. This delicious recipe is an excellent way of using up a lot of ripe mangoes (and its variation will help you to use up any unripe ones, too).*

Extract all the mango flesh, including that from the skins and the central seed. Put the flesh in a blender with the Cointreau and cream and blend for 30–45 seconds.

Pour into either a large dessert serving bowl or into individual dessert glasses. Chill until set. Before serving, decorate as desired with sprigs of fresh mint, glacé fruit or fresh fruit.

*Note:* A variation of this recipe is to use unripe or semi-ripe mangoes. Peel the mangoes and slice off all the flesh. Put in a pot with a small amount of water — 9 mL (3 fl oz) for every 5–7 mangoes. Cook the mango flesh until soft and blend together with 15 g (1 tablespoon) of sugar to every 5 mangoes. Chill and serve with cream.

SERVES 6–8

# MALI

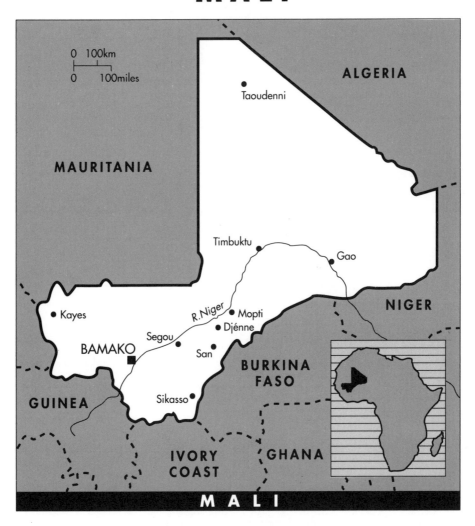

**Official title**   Republic of Mali

**Capital city**   Bamako

**Official language**   French

**Currency**   CFA francs = 100 centimes

**Cash crops for export**   Groundnuts (peanuts), cereals, cotton, fresh fruits, vegetables, livestock and fish

**Food crops**   Rice, maize, millet, sorghum, groundnuts and vegetables. Recurrent drought has caused a regular food deficit.

**Total land area**   Approximately 1,240,000 sq km

# MALIAN FISH STEW

**500 g (1 lb) salted, dried fish**

**1 L (1¾ pt) water**

**90 mL (3 fl oz) vegetable oil**

**3 large onions, finely chopped**

**2-3 red chillies (hot peppers), finely chopped (optional)**

**4 medium tomatoes, diced**

**15-20 okros (okras), cooked**

*Mali is a landlocked country which only has one fully navigable river, the Niger. So instead of the ocean fish available to their coastal neighbours, the Malians eat freshwater fish such as Tilapia and salted, dried fish such as that used in this recipe.*

Soak the fish overnight in some water. Drain off the water and wash off excess salt. Remove any bones from the fish. Put the fish in 750 mL (1¼ pt) water and bring to the boil. Lower the heat and simmer gently.

Heat the oil in a pot and fry half the onions and all the chillies (hot peppers) until golden. Add the tomatoes and cook for 3 minutes then stir in the remaining 250 mL (8 fl oz) water and simmer slowly for about 15 minutes.

Mash the remaining onion with the okro (okra) and add to the fish. Stir and simmer for 20–30 minutes until the fish has softened and the water has reduced a little. Combine the onion/tomato/chilli (hot pepper) mixture with the fish mixture and serve with Fufu (page 13) or some other type of dumpling (e.g. page 24).

SERVES 4

## THE LAND OF THE HIPPOPOTAMUS

The name Mali first appeared some six centuries ago and is thought to have derived from the Mandingo word meaning hippopotamus.

▼▼▼

# KYINKYINGA
WEST AFRICAN KEBABS

1 kg (2 lb) medium lean steak or liver

3 medium green capsicums (sweet or bell peppers), halved, seeded and cut into 2.5 cm (1 in) squares

30 g (1 oz) unsalted, dry-roasted groundnuts (peanuts) ground to powder in a coffee grinder or with a mortar and pestle

*SEASONING*

4 medium onions, diced

10 g (2 teaspoons) grated root ginger

30 g (1 oz) plain flour

60 g (2 oz) unsalted, dry-roasted groundnuts (peanuts) ground to powder

2 large overripe tomatoes, blanched, peeled and mashed

15 g (1 tablespoon) garlic salt

15 mL (1 tablespoon) fresh Chilli Sambal (page 22–23) Tabasco sauce or chilli paste (e.g. Sambal Oelek)

*Like plantain and nuts, Kyinkyinga (pronounced 'chinchinga') is 'street' food and a vendor's delight. Because these moist, seasoned skewers of meat and capsicum (sweet or bell pepper) attract flies, Kyinkyinga is kept in closed glass cabinets which are perched precariously on the vendors' heads.*

*The vendors rush into traffic stopped at red lights or up to buses and lorries parked at rest stops to try to make a quick sale. The acrobatics involved in balancing a heavy glass case full of hot Kyinkyinga while simultaneously counting change from a money belt defies description!*

Remove excess fat from meat, wipe with a clean damp cloth or paper towel and cut into bite-sized cubes. Mix all ingredients for seasoning together in a bowl. Combine the meat and half the seasoning and mix thoroughly. Stand for a minimum of 1 hour before grilling. Skewer the seasoned meat alternately with the green capsicums (sweet or bell peppers) and grill until cooked and browned both sides. If liver is used, be careful not to overcook and dry it out.

Remove from the heat and sprinkle with the remaining 30 g (1 oz) of the groundnut (peanut) powder. Serve with salad, rice, bread or by itself. Leftover seasoning can be made into a sauce: add 60 mL (2 fl oz) wine (moselle or ginger wine) and heat to thicken, then pour over the kebabs. You can make the sauce thinner by adding more wine.

SERVES 4

# MAAFE

CHICKEN AND GROUNDNUT (PEANUT) STEW

**Groundnut (peanut) oil**

**3 medium onions, finely diced**

**1 whole chicken, cleaned and jointed**

**Salt to taste**

**2 red chillies (hot peppers), finely chopped**

**4 medium tomatoes blanched, peeled and diced**

**30 g (2 tablespoons) tomato paste blended with 60 mL (4 table-spoons) water**

**750 mL (1¼ pt) boiling water**

**250 mL (8 fl oz) smooth groundnut (peanut) paste**

**8 okro (okra), topped and tailed**

**2 sweet potatoes or yams, peeled and cut into 5 cm (2 in) cubes**

**250 g (½ lb) corn (maize) kernels**

**4 carrots, cut into 4–6 chunks**

**Spinach (silver beet), turnips or other firm, root vegetable of your choice**

**Pinch each of ground cinnamon and paprika**

*Like Palava Sauce, the origins of Maafe have been lost. Because it tastes so wonderful and is so easy to make, a number of West African countries have claimed it as their own, each adding a regional stamp to the basic recipe. However, I feel pretty certain that it is the Bambara people of Mali who deserve the credit for this chicken and nut stew.*

Heat the oil in a large, heavy-based pot and sauté the onions, and the chicken pieces seasoned with salt until the chicken is sealed and browned. Stir in the chillies (hot peppers), tomatoes and blended tomato paste. Blend the boiling water and the groundnut (peanut) paste together until smooth and add to the pot. Stir and simmer for 40 minutes.

Add all the vegetables, the cinnamon and paprika, and season with some salt. Stir well and simmer gently on low heat until the chicken is cooked, the volume reduced and the sauce thick. Serve hot with rice, potato croquettes or cooked root vegetables.

SERVES 4

# AKARA
FRIED BEAN BALLS

250 g (½ lb) black-eyed beans

1–2 red chillies (hot peppers), finely diced

1 medium onion, finely diced

5 g (1 teaspoon) salt

2 eggs

125 mL (4 fl oz) water

Salt to taste

Groundnut (peanut) or other vegetable oil for deep-frying

*Beans are a common ingredient in the diet of many African people including those who have moved west to the Caribbean and beyond. The black-eyed variety, from which Akara (or Koosé as it is also known) is made, is a versatile and wonderful favourite. Akara is one of many recipes taken to the West Indies during the iniquitous slave trade. To this day Akara is called 'Akkra' in Jamaica; 'Accra' in Trinidad and Tobago; but 'Calas' in New Orleans!*

*These fried bean balls are light and tasty and the recipe is common throughout West Africa, particularly among Muslims. Fastidious cooks go to the trouble of skinning the beans before mashing them for cooking, but I feel as though I am losing the quality and colour if I do that. It's up to you.*

Soak the beans overnight in 1L (1¾ pt) cold water. There are two methods of preparing the beans. If you decide to use the peeling method, alternately thresh the soaked beans between your palms and rinse them in water so the skins wash away. Repeat the process until all the beans are skinned and you are left with white beans. Alternatively, if you choose not to peel the beans then you simply rinse them several times.

Blend the beans in small batches, adding small amounts of the water to make it easier. Blend the first batch of beans with the chilli (hot pepper), onion, salt and eggs. When all the beans are blended, combine the thick puréed mixture in a bowl, adjust the seasoning and whisk for 3–4 minutes with a hand whisk to aerate the mixture.

Heat the oil in a deep frypan until it is very hot. With clean wet hands, form balls of mixture and gently drop them into the oil and fry until golden brown. Be careful the oil does not splash your hands. You may prefer to use a long-handled spoon. Fry the balls quickly in batches and drain them in a wire sieve lined with paper towels. Serve hot or cold.

SERVES 4–6

# KULIKULI
GROUNDNUT (PEANUT) BISCUITS

**500 g (1 lb) freshly ground groundnut (peanut) paste**

**125 mL (4 fl oz) warm water**

**Salt to taste**

**Groundnut (peanut) oil for deep-frying**

*This is another delicious groundnut (peanut) dish. Tasty and nutritious, it is frequently eaten as a snack or broken into croutons for a salad. Kulikuli (pronounced 'cooli-cooli') has an added benefit — it is frequently used in Africa as a rusk for teething babies, giving them something to rub against their gums.*

Groundnuts (peanuts) can often be freshly ground for you at health food shops. Put the groundnut (peanut) paste in a bowl and, using your hand, knead and squeeze the paste to coax out excess oil. Add small amounts of the warm water from time to time to aid in extracting the oil. Continue the kneading and squeezing process until most of the oil is extracted and you get a smooth paste. Add salt to taste. Add the extracted oil to the quantity already set aside for deep-frying.

Shape the remaining paste into rings or small, flat biscuits and fry until golden brown. Remove from the heat, drain and store until needed.

SERVES 4

## TIMBUKTU: REALITY OR MYTH?

During medieval times Mali was the most important trading area in the Islamic world. It was the seat of ancient empires based on the trade routes across the Sahara, the trade routes upon which cities such as Djenne, Timbuktu and Gao built their wealth.

These days 'Timbuktu' represents any distant, almost mythical place, but this ancient Malian city was founded in the eleventh century and at its most prosperous became a renowned gold trading centre as well as an intellectual centre of philosophy, learning and Islamic culture.

# JOLLOF RICE

500 g (1 lb) lean beef or chicken

Salt and ground white pepper, to taste

Vegetable oil for frying

1L (1¾ pt) stock or water with 3 crushed stockcubes

3 large onions, finely chopped

4 cloves garlic, peeled and finely chopped

2-3 chillies (hot peppers), finely chopped

4 large tomatoes, blanched, peeled and blended or mashed

45 g (3 tablespoons) tomato paste

250 g (8 oz) each of assorted chopped vegetables, e.g. carrots, green beans, mushrooms and capsicums (sweet or bell peppers)

500 g (1 lb) long-grain rice

Lettuce, parsley or fresh coriander (cilantro) and hard-boiled eggs to garnish

*Jollof Rice is among the best known of West African dishes not only because it is delicious and easy to prepare, but because the ingredients are readily available in Western countries! Its origin, however, remains a bone of contention between several West African nations. There are many regional cooking variations — this version is my mother's!*

Cut meat or chicken into 5 cm (2 in) cubes or small pieces and season with salt and pepper. Cover and allow to stand for 1–2 hours.

Heat oil in fry-pan and fry the meat or chicken pieces until brown. Remove meat from oil and add to the stock in a large, heavy-based saucepan. Simmer on low heat until meat begins to soften, then remove from heat.

Drain excess oil from frypan leaving enough oil to fry onions, garlic and chillies (hot peppers) until golden. Add tomatoes, tomato paste, half the combined vegetables and 250 mL (8 fl oz) of stock from the meat mixture. Stir well, adjust seasoning and simmer on low heat for 5–7 minutes. Add this vegetable sauce to the meat mixture in the saucepan and simmer gently. Finally, stir in the uncooked, long-grain rice. Adjust the seasoning again, cover and simmer slowly on low heat for about 15 minutes.

Arrange the remaining vegetables on top of the rice and continue to simmer until the rice absorbs all the stock, softens and cooks, and the meat is tender. It may be necessary to sprinkle additional water mix to help the rice cook. If so use small amounts at a time of approximately 250 mL (8 fl oz) lightly salted water.

Serve hot, garnished with chopped lettuce, parsley or fresh coriander (cilantro) and hard-boiled eggs.

SERVES 4–6

# MAASA
## SWEET MILLET FRITTERS

90 mL (3 fl oz) milk

90 mL (3 fl oz) water

15 g (1 tablespoon) caster sugar

10-15 g (2-3 teaspoons) dry yeast

250 g (½ lb) millet flour

250 g (½ lb) brown rice flour

15 g (1 tablespoon) baking powder

Vegetable oil

Icing sugar to taste

*Mali is a country where no food can be wasted. It does not have the bounty of the sea to rely on and, being an inland nation, does not have the more temperate climate of some of the coastal fringes. Drought can devastate the grain and vegetable crops that form an extensive part of the Malian diet.*

*Maasa (pronounced 'mah-sah') are millet fritters which can be served as a sweet snack or to accompany porridge at breakfast. In Mali, Maasa also uses broken rice unsuited to other rice dishes. The rice is ground and mixed with the millet flour, sugar, yeast and oil. The choice of brown rice flour increases the vitamin and fibre content.*

Combine the milk and water in a pan and heat gently. Pour into a mixing bowl and stir in the caster sugar to dissolve it. Add the yeast and keep the mixture warm (e.g. on top of a warm oven) and let it stand until the yeast becomes frothy.

Sift the millet flour, rice flour and baking powder together. Stir in the yeast mixture, cover and leave to rise for 30–40 minutes.

Stir the mixture gently but briefly. It should be the consistency of a thick pancake mix. Fry spoonfuls of the mixture in shallow, hot oil over low heat, turning frequently to prevent burning and to allow the Maasa to cook well right through.

Drain on paper towels and sprinkle with extra caster sugar.

Serve as a snack, a light meal or, without the sugar with soups or as a breakfast dish.

MAKES 16–20 PIECES

# LEMON GRASS TEA

**1.25 L (2 pt) water**

**250 g (½ lb) lemon grass, well washed with roots trimmed off, and then cut the grass into 5 cm (2 in) lengths**

**Sugar to taste**

*Herb teas are very popular in West Africa and this local favourite is poured from long-spouted, ornate, brass teapots into small tea cups with no handles. It is an excellent palate cleanser after a meal.*

Bring the water to the boil. Rinse out the brass teapot twice with small amounts of boiling water then add the lemon grass and pour in the rest of the boiling water.

Allow to brew for a while, depending on how strong a tea you prefer. Pour the hot tea into small handleless cups and serve with or without sugar. It tastes better without milk.

---

## DISHES OF GOLD

As a trading centre, Mali's wealth derived from taxes and customs duties. The kings of the old empire levied fees on every item that passed through the region.

So rich were the early kings that it is said that King Mansa Musa ruined the value of the Egyptian currency during a visit to Mecca in 1324 because he spent and bartered so much in gold.

Although in recent times Mali has been badly affected by drought and hardship, what apparent wealth there is appears as gold — much worn as jewellery. The goldsmiths of Mali can fashion exquisite, light but enormous earrings which can only be removed by melting down the earpiece. It is said that the people of Mali have dishes of gold but no food to put on them!

# MOROCCO

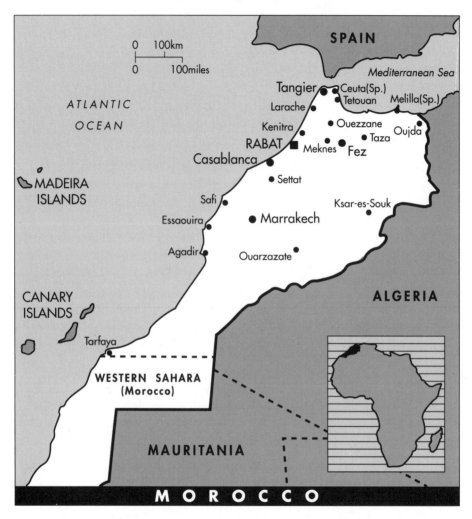

**Official title**    Kingdom of Morocco (known in Arabic as Al Mamlaka Al Maghrebia)

**Capital city**    Rabat (means 'Place of Faith')

**Official language**    Arabic, although French, Berber and Spanish are widely spoken

**Currency**    Moroccan dirham (DH) = 100 francs

**Cash crops for export**    Sugarcane, sugar beet, cotton and sardines. Livestock productivity and crop yields are generally low.

**Food crops**    Barley, wheat, maize, chickpeas, beans, olives, oilseeds, tomatoes, citrus fruit, potatoes and other vegetables

**Total land area**    Approximately 771,000 sq km

# POISSON SALÉ
## SALTED FISH

1 kg (2 lb) dry salted fish of your choice

60 mL (4 tablespoons) vegetable oil

1 large onion, finely chopped

2 cloves garlic, finely chopped

6 medium tomatoes, coarsely chopped

5 g (1 teaspoon) saffron

5 g (1 teaspoon) chilli (hot pepper) powder or paprika (optional)

250 mL (8 fl oz) water

1 green capsicum (sweet or bell pepper), coarsely chopped

1 red capsicum (sweet or bell pepper), coarsely chopped

125 g (4 oz) green beans coarsely chopped

Juice of ½ lemon (optional)

*Moroccans do not eat much fish, but when they do it is cooked in a French style.*

Soak the salted fish overnight in water to cover then remove the skin, if any, and any bones.

In a saucepan, combine the oil, onion, garlic, tomatoes, saffron, chilli (hot pepper) powder or paprika, and water. Bring to the boil on low heat and simmer for 5 minutes. Flake the fish into chunks and add to the sauce. Mix together taking care not to break up the fish pieces too much. Adjust the seasoning to taste.

Add the remaining vegetables and continue simmering on low heat for 10–15 minutes until the liquid reduces and the vegetables and fish are soft and cooked. Add lemon juice. Serve hot over rice or Couscous (page 52).

SERVES 4

# BSTILLA
## PIGEON PIE

*TOP LAYER*
**30 mL (2 tablespoons) vegetable oil**
**250 g (½ lb) blanched almonds**
**5 g (1 teaspoon) cinnamon**
**60 g (2 oz) brown or caster sugar**

*FILLING*
**125 g (4 oz) butter**
**1 large onion, finely diced**
**Flesh of 3–4 pigeons, boned and cut into chunks or use skinless meat from 1 whole chicken**
**½ teaspoon each: cinnamon, ground black pepper, paprika, ground ginger, mixed spice and saffron or turmeric**
**7 g (1½ teaspoons) salt**
**1 bunch each fresh coriander (cilantro) and parsley, finely chopped**
**375 mL (13 fl oz) water**
**6–8 eggs, beaten**

*FOR THE PIE*
**250 g (½ lb) butter, melted**
**14–16 sheets of filo pastry**
**60 g (4 tablespoons) icing sugar mixed with ½ teaspoon cinnamon**

*Pronounced 'pastilla', this combination savoury and sweet pie is a specialty of the Fassi (the inhabitants of Fez), although it is believed to have originated in Andalucia in southern Spain.*

*Traditionally Bstilla is served as one of several courses at a feast and is eaten with the fingers from a communal bowl. The pie is painstaking to prepare, so allow plenty of time — but the result is delicious and impressive.*

To prepare the top layer, heat the oil in a heavy-based frypan and brown the almonds. Drain the almonds and grind them to medium coarseness in a coffee grinder, or use a rolling pin and sheets of greaseproof paper. Combine the ground almonds with cinnamon and sugar, cover, and set aside.

To prepare the filling, melt the butter in a heavy-based saucepan, and fry the onion for 5–7 minutes. Stir in the meat, all the spices, salt, fresh coriander (cilantro) and parsley, and water. Cover and simmer on low heat for 15–20 minutes or until the meat is well cooked. Remove the meat from the sauce which by now should be reduced to about 250 mL (8 fl oz). Set aside the meat. Gradually add the eggs to the sauce, on low heat, stirring continuously until everything is well combined. Stir well, adjust the seasonings then remove from the heat.

To assemble the pie, lightly grease a deep 25–30 cm (10–12 in) diameter baking tray. Line the tray with 5–6 sheets of filo pastry working from the centre outwards, in a circular, clockwise manner. Brush each pastry sheet with melted butter before overlapping it with the next one. When completed, the pastry should overlap in the middle and overhang the edges of the tray. Lightly brush all over this pastry lining again with melted butter. Repeat the process of pastry laying to gain a second, thicker layer. Brush this too with melted butter.

Scoop the spicy sauce evenly into an inner 25 cm (10 in) circle of the layered pastry (if there is sauce left over, save the remainder for later). Cover this circle of sauce with another sheet of pastry, making sure this top layer fits only the inner

**From Mali** Kyinkyinga (Kebabs) (page 39)

**From Mali** Jollof Rice (page 43) with roast chicken

25 cm (10 in) circle by gently tucking the pastry edges under the sauce. Brush the top of this pastry with melted butter.

Arrange the sautéed pigeon or chicken and any leftover sauce on top of this layer of pastry. Brush 2 sheets of pastry with melted butter and cover the meat with them, laying them buttered side down, then brush the top with more melted butter. Spread the spicy, sugar and almond mixture evenly over the top of this pastry. Fold the pastry overhanging the dish inwards to cover the almond mix. Place another sheet of pastry on top, buttered side down. Brush the top again, with more melted butter.

If you have any more pastry left, gently lift up the pie and wrap it like a parcel in an overlapping circular manner as in the very beginning, tucking the edges under until the pastry sheets meet up and pie is all wrapped up. Brush the pie all over with remaining melted butter. The pie should now resemble a loaf of bread ready to be baked.

Bake in a preheated oven at 200°C (400°F) for 20–25 minutes until the top has browned nicely but the pie is still uncooked. Remove it from the oven and place a larger circular ovenproof dish over the pie and carefully turn it upside down. Return it to the oven for another 20–25 minutes to brown the bottom side of the pie as well. Using the same 'turning over' process, carefully turn the pie over again onto its bottom. Bake for a further 5–10 minutes which should allow the Bstilla to look golden brown and to be cooked on the inside.

Remove the Bstilla from the oven and place on a flat serving dish. Cut 8 thin strips of paper 1.5 cm (½ in) wide and 30 cm (12 in) long. Place these in a criss-cross fashion on top of the Bstilla, 4 one way and 4 across them to form diamond shapes. To decorate, put the icing sugar and cinnamon mix in a sieve and rub it through the holes onto the criss-crossed top of the Bstilla. When this is done, carefully lift off the strips of paper. The end result should look like a brown-and-white diamond grid and should justify all the effort. Serve hot. This is a meal fit for a king!

SERVES 4–6

# TAGINE OF CHICKEN WITH PRUNES

**6 large chicken pieces**
**3 onions, 1 sliced into thin rings and 2 finely diced**
**1 teaspoon saffron**
**1½ teaspoons grated root ginger**
**Salt to taste**
**375 g (12 oz) pitted prunes**
**1 L (1 ¾ pt) water**

*This Tagine, a variety of stew, is made with chicken and prunes with the spiciness of ginger and colouring of saffron. The recipe is said to be very old — one of the oldest in this region of Africa.*

Combine the chicken, diced onions, saffron, ginger, salt, half the prunes, and water in a large saucepan. Cover and simmer gently over low heat. Turn the chicken periodically and stir occasionally. After the first hour of cooking, arrange the sliced onions on top of the chicken pieces. Arrange the remaining prunes around the chicken, and continue to cook uncovered on low heat for another 30 minutes. Add small amounts of water if the original stock reduces too quickly before the chicken is cooked. Be careful not to add too much water, as the sauce should be plentiful but thick.

Adjust the seasoning to taste. When the chicken is cooked, the prunes are soft and the stock is thick, serve hot with either Couscous (page 52) or boiled rice and vegetables of your choice.

SERVES 4–6

## THE MOROCCAN MELTING POT

Morocco is the closest country to Europe on the African continent. It is the place where Arabia and Africa and Europe merge. The people and culture are an exotic blend of the Berbers (the indigenous people) who live in the mountain villages, the Arab-speaking majority who live in the towns of the lowlands, and a European (mainly French) population. Morocco is a place of great natural beauty — from the soaring Atlas Mountains to the beautiful beaches of the Atlantic and Mediterranean coasts. It is also an area of great historical significance with the ancient walled city of Fez founded in 808 AD. The dishes to be found here reflect a long history of centuries of different peoples and their civilisations.

# TAGINE OF LAMB WITH PUMPKINS VEGETABLES AND FRUIT

**1 kg (2 lb) stewing lamb, roughly chopped**

**4 cloves garlic, finely chopped**

**2 small onions, peeled and coarsely chopped**

**Salt to taste**

**5 g (1 teaspoon) cayenne pepper**

**60 mL (4 tablespoons) vegetable oil**

**15 g (3 teaspoons) turmeric**

**8-10 large tomatoes, blanched, peeled and diced**

**1-2 red chillies (hot peppers), optional**

**15 g (1 tablespoon) raisins**

**500 g (1 lb) pumpkin, peeled and coarsely chopped**

**1 kg (2 lb) green beans, halved**

**Juice of ½ lemon**

*The Sahara forms a kind of culinary barrier as well as a physical one. North of the desert it is common to use sugar, vinegar and fruit in savoury dishes, an example of European influences.*

*South of the Sahara, however, to combine sweet and sour flavours is to breach a number of tribal taboos. Ashanti (from Ghana) and Tanzanian men, for example, believe that to eat too much sugary food is effeminate and can even affect their sexual prowess!*

*As well as fruits, Moroccan cooks use an enormous range of spices in their cooking to give a pungent flavour, aroma and colour to their food. Touajan (the plural of Tagine) are boiled or steamed since the Moroccans prefer foods to cook in their own juices rather than to fry them.*

Preheat the oven to 180°C (350°F). Combine the meat, garlic, onions, salt, pepper, oil, turmeric, tomatoes and chillies (hot peppers) in a deep baking dish. Mix well by stirring. Cover and bake for about 45 minutes. Add the raisins and cook for another 15 minutes. Stir in the pumpkin, beans and lemon juice, cover again and cook for a further 1–1½ hours until the meat is tender and cooked. Serve hot with Couscous (page 52) or Saffron Rice (page 54).

SERVES 4–6

# PLAIN COUSCOUS

**375 g (¾ lb) dry couscous**
**500 mL (¾ pt) cold water**
**¼–½ teaspoon salt to taste**
**10 g (2 teaspoons) cinnamon**
**30 mL (2 tablespoons) vegetable oil**
**15 g (1 tablespoon) butter**

*The most well known of the Magreb dishes, couscous is believed to be Berber in origin. Although it is one of the national foods of Morocco, its preparation varies widely from region to region, ranging from plain to sweet couscous, with vegetables or meat in between.*

*Made from durum wheat semolina, couscous is best prepared in a couscousiere, a specially designed steamer. If, however, you do not own one, a combined saucepan and steamer will work well. The recipe below is for cooking loose couscous. Precooked varieties or 'couscous rapide' are also available at supermarkets and health food stores.*

In a large bowl combine the couscous and water, stir well and leave to soak for 10–15 minutes. Pour the couscous and water out through a large tea towel or muslin cloth and squeeze out most of the water from the couscous. Pour the wet couscous onto a tray, fluff out the grains with a fork, cover and leave a further 15 minutes to swell up. Bring enough water to the boil in the saucepan of a double boiler. Tip the couscous into the top saucepan, spread out the couscous grains as much as possible, place saucepan on top of the boiling water and steam uncovered. Alternatively, if you are serving couscous with a stew, place the couscous over the stew and heat.

Steam the couscous for 20–30 minutes then tip it out onto a wide tray, separate the grains with a fork, and cool it for 10 minutes. Using your fingers, rub the salt, cinnamon and oil through the grains to separate them further. Return the couscous to the steamer a second time and steam, partially covered, for 20–30 minutes more until it softens and tastes cooked. Remove the couscous from the steamer and pour onto the tray again. Stir in the butter and fluff out the grains with two forks.

Serve hot with any of the tagines or stews in this book or any other vegetables, stews or roast dishes of your choice. Try adding cooked chick peas or raisins for variety.

SERVES 4–6

# SWEET COUSCOUS

500 g (1 lb) hot, steamed couscous

125 g (4 oz) raisins

90 g (3 oz) caster sugar

30 g (2 tablespoons) butter

2-4 drops aromatic rosewater or vanilla essence

250 mL (8 fl oz) milk or cream

Flowers to decorate (e.g. frangipani)

*Served in individual portions with milk or cream, this recipe, in which raisins, vanilla or rosewater and sugar are added, is eaten as a pudding in the Magreb countries of North Africa. It is yet another example of the versatility of couscous!*

Combine all the ingredients except the milk or cream in a large bowl and mix thoroughly. Warm the milk in a small pan over low heat without allowing it to boil. If you are using cream do not heat it.

Place small amounts of sweet couscous in individual bowls. Top with warm milk or cream and decorate each serving with a flower, like frangipani, to serve.

SERVES 4-6

## FEZ AND MARRAKESH

Fez, the oldest city of Morocco, and Marrakesh, one of the most mystical, are both ancient walled cities whose narrow, labyrinthine streets are full of long-held secrets waiting to be discovered. Wander along the ancient alleyways and through the archways of the souks and you will discover bazaars selling all sorts of crafts, jewellery and exotic, spicy foods. Here tourists, merchants, thieves and donkeys mingle and the spectacle — and sounds and smells — are not easily forgotten. Be wary though as you can soon lose your way.

# SAFFRON RICE

90 g (3 oz) butter

500 g (1 lb) long-grain white rice (preferably aromatic rice)

2 green capsicums (sweet or bell peppers), finely diced

5 g (1 teaspoon) saffron or 10 g (2 teaspoons) turmeric

5 g (1 teaspoon) salt

6 cardamom pods

5 g (1 teaspoon) paprika or cayenne pepper (optional)

1 L (1¾ pt) cold water

*Colourful and aromatic, this side dish is perfect to serve with stews and roasts. If saffron is unavailable, then substituting turmeric works almost as well. I also recommend you use aromatic rices such as basmati or jasmine.*

Melt the butter in a large, heavy-based saucepan on medium to low heat and fry the rice and capsicums (sweet or bell peppers), stirring intermittently for 15–20 minutes until the rice crisps and starts to brown. Add the saffron or turmeric, salt, cardamom pods, paprika or pepper and cold water. Stir well and simmer on low heat for 25–30 minutes or until all the water is absorbed and the rice is soft and cooked. You may need to add extra small amounts of salted water to the rice if it is still hard and uncooked after the allotted time. Fluff up the cooked rice with a fork, remove the cardamom pods and serve hot to accompany the stew or roast of your choice.

SERVES 6–8

# ALMOND MILK

185 g (6 oz) lightly roasted almonds finely ground in a coffee grinder

125 g (4 oz) brown or caster sugar

250 mL (8 fl oz) water

1 L (1¾ pt) milk

15 g (1 tablespoon) grated orange rind

*This drink is a Moroccan specialty, served all over the country as a complement to, or a change from, the Moroccan 'thé'. It is even available as 'street' food. A delicate combination of almonds and orange makes this a delicious beverage when chilled.*

In a bowl combine the almonds and the sugar and mix well. Add half the water and leave to soak for 30 minutes. Put in a blender and blend on low speed as you drizzle in the remaining water. Blend well and leave to stand for another 30 minutes.

Warm the milk slightly and stir in the orange rind. Strain in the almond mix to combine with the milk and rind. Stir well and serve immediately.

SERVES 4

# EGYPT

**Official title**    Arab Republic of Egypt (known in Arabic as Misr)

**Capital city**    Cairo (known in Arabic as Al Qahirah), the largest city in Africa and the Middle East

**Official languages**    Arabic, although English and French are widely spoken in business

**Currency**    Egyptian pound = 100 piastres

**Cash crops for export**    Cotton, sugarcane, sugar beet, berseem Egyptian clover, potatoes and tomatoes

**Food crops**    Maize, sorghum, rice, wheat, beans and vegetables

**Total land area**    Approximately 1,000,000 sq km

# MOLOHIA

500 g (1 lb) molohia leaves (available from specialty shops) or spinach (silver beet)

1 kg (2 lb) red meat or chicken meat, diced

1 large onion, finely diced

Salt and pepper to taste

1 L (1¾ pt) water

30 g (2 tablespoons) butter

10 cloves garlic, crushed

30 g (2 tablespoons) coriander (cilantro) powder

250 g (8 oz) boiled rice

15 mL (1 tablespoon) vinegar mixed with 1 finely chopped onion

Hot pita bread, cut in triangles

*Along with the much-loved Fuul Medames (page 63), Molohia is one of Egypt's national dishes. Pronounced 'mol-oh-hee-a', it is a thick green soup, particularly popular with the Egyptian Arabs. Molohia is the small green leaf (rather like a small-leafed spinach) of a plant of the Mallow family.*
*It is possible to substitute spinach (silver beet) leaves if molohia is unavailable.*

Wash and finely chop the molohia leaves (Egyptians usually use a double-handled metal chopper called 'makhrata' to do this) and set aside. Leave the fat on the meat and combine it in a pot with the diced onion, salt and pepper and 500 mL (¾ pt) water. Boil the meat until tender, about 30–40 minutes depending on whether you are using red meat or chicken. Remove the meat from the stock and set aside. Add the molohia or spinach (silver beet) leaves to the stock and boil for about 5 minutes.

Place the butter in a frypan and briefly fry the garlic and coriander (cilantro) for 1 minute only, without burning. Tip this mixture into the molohia or spinach (silver beet) and stock while the stock is still boiling. Be very careful, it may splatter but it smells fantastic.

Serve the soup hot accompanied by side dishes of the boiled meat, boiled rice, chopped onion and vinegar mix, and hot pita bread cut into triangles. Allow your guests to make their own selection and combinations.

SERVES 4

# 'BIRDS WITHIN BIRDS'

## FOWL
**1 quail, 1 spatchcock (baby chicken), 1 medium chicken, 1 large turkey**

## QUAIL
**10 g (2 teaspoons) tomato paste**

**60 mL (4 tablespoons) water**

**30 mL (2 tablespoons) vegetable oil**

**Freshly ground black pepper**

**10 g (2 teaspoons) ginger powder**

**Salt to taste**

**Saffron Egg (page 62)**

## SPATCHCOCK
**6 pitted prunes or dates**

**375 mL (13 fl oz) ginger wine, spicy mead or similar**

**30 mL (2 tablespoons) water**

## CHICKEN
**60 g (4 tablespoons) cumin powder**

**15 g (1 tablespoon) garlic salt**

**10 g (2 teaspoons) cayenne pepper, paprika or hot chilli powder (optional)**

**75 mL (2½ fl oz) vegetable oil**

*Once, in an old Middle Eastern cookbook belonging to a friend, I saw a recipe for stuffed camel. The idea was so bizarre and so charmed me that I just had to set about trying to create a manageable equivalent — without the camel! Instead I use poultry in a gradation of sizes: each bird is stuffed inside another (hence the name!) like Russian dolls. It is an impressive dish and makes a wonderful talking point, but it is not at all difficult to make, just time-consuming because of the lengthy preparation of the marinades and the cooking time of the individual birds.*

It is advisable to prepare and marinate the birds for 12–24 hours before cooking them because they taste better. Also, if you have a big enough oven, try to cook 2–3 birds, covered, at once to save time. Cook the turkey first as it takes the longest, then the chicken. The spatchcock and the quail can cook together.

To prepare the quail, combine the tomato paste and water to form a creamy mixture. Add the oil, black pepper, ginger and salt and stir well. Smear this marinade over the quail and inside. Pierce the quail with a sharp skewer so the marinade permeates the flesh. Cover and stand for 12 hours. When ready to cook, preheat the oven to 200°C (400°F). Wrap the quail in aluminium foil and bake in an oven dish for 15 minutes. Reduce the heat to 180°C (350°F) and bake for a further 40 minutes until the quail is tender. Remove from the oven, set aside and keep warm.

To prepare the spatchcock, soak the prunes or dates in ginger wine overnight. Mash them together to form a paste. Add the water and stir well. Smear this all over the spatchcock inside and out. Wrap it in aluminium foil and bake in the oven at 180–190°C (350°–370°F) for about 40 minutes until cooked. Remove from the heat, keep covered, set aside and keep warm.

To prepare the chicken, combine the cumin, garlic salt, cayenne pepper and oil in a bowl, and mix well. Coat the

*TURKEY*

**8–10 sprigs rosemary**

**90 g (3 oz) butter**

**15 g (1 tablespoon) garlic salt**

*ACCOMPANIMENTS*

**Roast potatoes in their jackets or peeled**

**Baked sweet potatoes in their jackets or peeled**

**Plain boiled rice**

**Turnips and parsnips roasted with the meat**

**Steamed broccoli, carrots, spinach (silver beet) or snow peas (mange tout)**

chicken inside and out with this, cover with aluminium foil and bake in a baking dish at 180°C (350°F) for approximately 1 hour or until chicken is cooked. Remove from the oven, set aside and keep warm.

To prepare the turkey, rub off the green spikes from the rosemary sprigs. Put these spikes into a bowl, with the butter and garlic salt, and blend well. Stuff the rosemary butter under as much of the turkey skin as possible. Rub the rest all over the turkey and on the inside as well. Cover with aluminium foil and bake according to weight.

By the last half hour of the cooking process, the chicken, spatchcock and quail should all be ready for stuffing. Remove the turkey from the oven. Remove the foil from the quail, spatchcock, chicken and the turkey. Stuff the Saffron Egg inside the quail, taking care not to squash either. Stuff the quail inside the spatchcock. Stuff the two inside the chicken and finally, stuff the lot inside the turkey, taking care at all stages not to let the birds disintegrate.

Brush the turkey with the pan juices and put it back into the oven without the foil cover. At this point, the vegetables could be added to cook in the juices in the pan. Continue baking at 180°C (350°F) for another 40–60 minutes.

When everything is cooked, place the 'stuffed up' turkey on a large serving dish and garnish elaborately with vegetables, and with flowers and foliage from your garden. This dish is best eaten in the typical African fashion: do not bother to carve neat little pieces; pull off pieces and share around, the idea is that as you get to each layer, a different taste sensation awaits you! Bon appétit.

SERVES 4–6

# NESTING PIGEONS

**6–8 pigeons cleaned and ready for roasting**

**90 mL (3 fl oz) olive oil**

**3 cloves garlic, finely chopped**

**Salt to taste**

*SALAD NEST*
**1 lettuce**
**1 cucumber, sliced**
**Snow peas (mange tout)**
**Alfalfa sprouts (lucerne)**
**Sunflower shoots**
**2 firm, ripe tomatoes, sliced into rounds**

*GARLIC SAUCE*
**4 cloves garlic, diced**
**2 eggs**
**5 g (1 teaspoon) mustard**
**375 mL (13 fl oz) vegetable oil**
**Juice of 1 lemon**
**1 loaf herb bread, warmed**

*Egyptians love eating pigeon, and in rural areas of the country, pigeons are specially bred for eating. The tall mud cotes are frequently to be seen on the roofs of their owners' houses. I have added my own variation to this quick lunchtime recipe, which is particularly appetising when served with a good, chilled white wine.*

To prepare the pigeons, mix the oil with the garlic and salt and rub over the pigeons, inside and out. Arrange the pigeons on a baking dish and bake in a preheated oven at 200°C (400°F) for about 1–1 ½ hours until the pigeons are cooked, brown and crispy skinned. Remove from the oven, drain on a wire rack and set aside.

To prepare the salad nest, wash the lettuce and separate the leaves. Arrange in a circular manner on a big serving tray. Arrange the cooked birds among the lettuce, add the cucumber slices, the snow peas (mange tout), and the sunflower shoots, all the time trying to camouflage the bodies of the birds so that their legs stick out. Sprinkle with the alfalfa sprouts (lucerne) and give it a red border by arranging the slices of tomato around the edge of the serving dish.

To prepare the sauce, put the garlic and eggs in a blender and blend well on medium to high setting for about 30 seconds, lower the setting slightly then add the mustard and blend again. With the machine running dribble the oil gently and evenly into the sauce until the mixture is thick and creamy. Finally, blend in the lemon juice. Pour the Garlic Sauce into a small bowl and serve with the warm or cold Nesting Pigeons or other poultry, meat or seafood.

SERVES 4–6

# KOFTA WITH TOMATO AND YOGHURT

500 g (1 lb) lean topside minced beef

6 cloves garlic, crushed

1 onion, diced

15 g (1 tablespoon) tomato paste

2 eggs

15 g (1 tablespoon) cumin powder

Salt and pepper to taste

Vegetable oil for deep-frying

10-12 medium tomatoes, blanched, peeled and seeded

125 mL (4 fl oz) plain yoghurt

4 red chillies (hot peppers)

*Minced meat or kofta is eaten widely in Egypt and the rest of the Middle East. This recipe is the one my mother calls her simple 'Pharaoh' dish: 'simple' because it is so easy to make; and 'Pharaoh' because it is a dish for kings — and it's Egyptian!*

In a deep bowl, combine the meat, garlic, onion, tomato paste, eggs, cumin, salt and pepper to taste. Mix thoroughly together. Form into small balls the size of table tennis balls.

Heat the oil in a deep frypan. Fry the meatballs in batches and set aside. Blend or process the tomatoes to a purée. Put the fried meatballs in a saucepan, pour over the tomato purée, stir, season to taste and simmer gently for 10–15 minutes.

Serve with bowls of plain yoghurt and freshly chopped chillies (hot peppers). Accompany with rice, couscous (page 52), yam balls and steamed spinach (silver beet).

SERVES 4–6

## PROVIDING FOR THE AFTERLIFE

For centuries the wonders of Egypt (the United Arab Republic) have held great fascination for historians and travellers from all over the world. Who has not heard of the Pyramids, the Sphinx, the bustling city of Cairo or the lifeblood of Egypt, the Nile?

Many African influences can be found in the Egyptian culture and lifestyle and it is now known that the Egyptians made trade missions as far as the rainforests of the Congo in West Africa during the early Egyptian kingdoms. Some Egyptian food is common to the whole North African and Middle Eastern region. Since the days of the pharaohs, here, as elsewhere in Africa, food played a large part in funerary rites. All over Egypt the tombs of kings, queens and nobles have been opened to reveal rich provision for the afterlife — from all kinds of foods to casks of wine and beer.

# BAMIA

OKRO (OKRA) AND LAMB STEW

**1 kg (2 lb) fresh okros (okras)**

**3 onions, finely chopped**

**4 cloves garlic, chopped**

**90 mL (3 fl oz) vegetable oil or samna (Egyptian rich clarified butter)**

**1.5 kg (3 lb) lamb, cubed**

**Salt and pepper to taste**

**250 g (½ lb) tomatoes, blanched, peeled and diced**

**10 g (2 teaspoons) tomato paste mixed with 250 mL (8 fl oz) water**

**1 sprig fresh coriander (cilantro)**

**Juice of 1 lemon, optional**

*All my friends treasure this stew – and I can understand why, as it is close to my favourite native Ghanaian dish, Okro (Okra) Stew (page 20). Increasingly, people are using veal and beef in this recipe, but I prefer the tradition and flavour of lamb.*

Top and tail the okros (okras), wash thoroughly and slice into 0.5 cm (¼ in) thick rings. Do not remove the seeds. In a heavy-based saucepan, fry the onions and garlic in the oil or samna until they start to brown. Add the lamb and season to taste. Stir well and cook until meat also starts to brown. Stir in the okros (okras) and continue cooking for 10–15 minutes on low heat until the okros (okras) begin to soften. Add the tomatoes with the tomato paste blended with water. You may need to add more water later.

Stir well, adjust the seasoning to taste and simmer slowly for 40 minutes until the meat is tender, the vegetables are cooked and the sauce is a thick and creamy consistency. Add the coriander (cilantro) and the lemon juice. Serve hot with rice or couscous (page 52).

SERVES 4

# SULIMAN'S PILAFF

215 mL (7 fl oz) vegetable oil

500 g (1 lb) rice

500 mL (¾ pt) boiling water

Salt and pepper to taste

500 g (1 lb) mutton or leftover roast meat

2 onions, diced

4 cloves garlic, diced

6–7 small tomatoes, blanched, peeled and diced

125 g (4 oz) each raisins, currants and pinenuts

*Suliman was an ancient Arab ruler: my Egyptian friend Beatrice named this favourite recipe of hers after Suliman in the belief that a pilaff named in this way assures the eater of a dish that is rich, exotic and mysterious.*

In a heavy-based saucepan heat 125 mL (4 fl oz) oil. When hot, add the rice, stirring for 4-5 minutes until the rice looks 'transparent'. Pour in enough boiling water to cover the rice. Add salt to taste, cover and simmer on low heat for about 20 minutes, being careful not to overcook.

In a separate saucepan, heat the remaining 90 mL (3 fl oz) oil. Fry the mutton, onions, garlic, tomatoes, raisins, currants and pinenuts for about 10 minutes, stirring constantly. Season to taste.

Stir this mixture into the rice in the heavy-based pan. (You may need to add some extra water here to help the rice soften). Cover and simmer on low heat for about 20 minutes or until the rice and meat are cooked, and the rice has absorbed all the stock. Serve hot accompanied by bowls of plain yoghurt, cucumber, sliced tomato and onion, green capsicum (sweet or bell peppers), red chillies (hot peppers) and browned pinenuts (brown quickly in a saucepan with a very thin film of oil).

SERVES 4–6

## SAFFRON EGGS

Saffron Eggs are cooked using a similar method to Hamine Eggs (see opposite page). As a decorative addition to many dishes hardboil 4 eggs, then cool in cold water and peel. Put ½ teaspoon of saffron into a saucepan filled with hot water, add the eggs, and slowly bring to the boil again. Boil for approximately 5–10 minutes, strain, cool and serve as usual. The eggs absorb the colour of the saffron and look very pretty. The recipe 'Birds Within Birds' (pages 57–58) uses a Saffron Egg as part of the dish.

# FUUL MEDAMES

**500 g (1 lb) Fuul Medames beans, soaked overnight**

*DRESSING*
**2–3 cloves garlic, crushed**
**9 mL (3 fl oz) olive oil**
**Salt and pepper to taste**
**Juice from 2 lemons**

*HAMINE EGGS*
**Brown onion skins**
**4 white eggs**

*GARNISH*
**250 g (½ lb) chopped parsley**
**Pitted black olives**

*Made from broad brown Fuul Medames beans and Hamine Eggs, this is one of Egypt's oldest dishes, said to date back to the Pharaohs. Due to its versatility and great popularity, it has remained one of Egypt's most celebrated national dishes. There are a number of variations on the basic recipe, and it can be used as a dip or a spread. The Fuul Medames beans can be bought from most Middle Eastern and Greek delicatessens. Brown kidney beans can be used as a substitute, but the flavour is not as authentic as traditional Fuul Medames.*

*The Hamine Eggs are hard boiled, slowly cooked in a juice or stew which lends colouring to the shells and flavour to the whites and yokes. An enduring cultural tradition, it is common practice in Egypt to cook eggs still in their shells in stews.*

Rinse the soaked beans two or three times in water and place in a large saucepan. Boil the beans in fresh water for 2 hours until tender. The beans should mash easily when squashed between fingers and there should be little or no water left when the beans are cooked. You may need to add more boiling water periodically during the cooking process. It is quite common to boil the eggs in with the beans, but some people prefer to pressure-cook their beans.

Remove the beans from the heat and cool. Partially mash them. Mix together the garlic, olive oil, salt, pepper and lemon juice to form a dressing.

To cook the eggs, combine brown onions skins, white eggs and enough water to boil for some time. Bring to the boil on very low heat and boil until the eggs go brown.

Spread a little mashed bean onto the centre of a plate, peel an egg and stand it in the middle of the bean paste, top with some garlic dressing and sprinkle some parsley on top. Garnish with the black olives. Serve accompanied by warm, herb or other bread. Some people add lentils and other pulses to their Fuul Medames.

SERVES 4–6

# ETHIOPIA

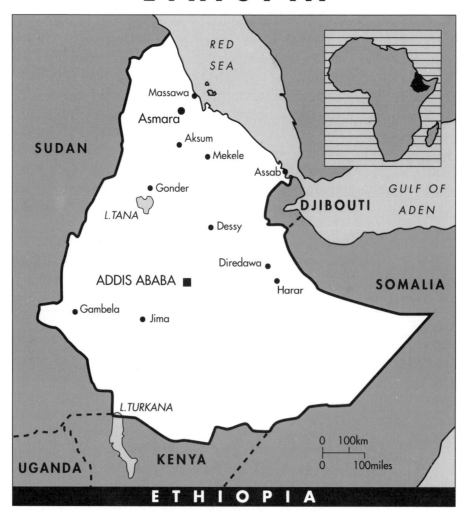

RED SEA

Massawa
Asmara
Aksum
Mekele
Assab
Gonder
L.TANA
Dessy
Diredawa
ADDIS ABABA ■
Harar
Gambela
Jima
L.TURKANA

SUDAN

DJIBOUTI

GULF OF ADEN

SOMALIA

KENYA

UGANDA

0    100km
0    100miles

ETHIOPIA

**Official title**   Republic of Ethiopia

**Capital city**   Addis Ababa (means 'New Flower' in Amharic)

**Official languages**   Amharic and English

**Currency**   Ethiopian Birr = 100 cents

**Cash crops for export**   Coffee, sugar and cotton. Due to persistent drought and war, food has been severely depleted.

**Food crops**   Under normal circumstances, maize, teff (local cereal), sorghum, millet, wheat and livestock are readily available

**Total land area**   Approximately 1,250,000 sq km

64

**From Morocco** Tagine of Lamb and Pumpkin, Vegetables and Fruit (page 51) with Couscous (page 52)

**From Ivory Coast and Morocco**   Mango Fool (page 36), dried figs, and Almond Milk (page 54)

# ETHIOPIAN FISH

**4 medium, salted fish**

**4 cloves garlic, crushed**

**2 teaspoons Berbere mix (see page 70)**

**4 large tomatoes, sliced**

**45 mL (3 tablespoons), groundnut (peanut) oil**

**Dry, ground groundnuts (peanuts) (optional)**

*Many of the dishes I have included from Ethiopia use a local seasoning called 'Berbere' (pronounced bari baray), a combination of dry, hot spices frequently used in stews. I have given the recipe for Berbere on page 70.*

*It is the combination of salted fish and Berbere that makes this simple dish so delicious.*

Soak the salted fish in water overnight to remove excess salt. Rinse the fish well and soak for 10 minutes in a bowl of boiling water. Lightly grease a baking dish, carefully lift out each fish and place it in the dish.

On each fish sprinkle some crushed garlic, 1/2 teaspoon of Berbere mix, slices from 1 tomato with slices arranged down the length of the fish, 10 mL (2 teaspoons) of groundnut (peanut) oil and a sprinkling of dry groundnuts (peanuts).

Cover and bake in a preheated oven at 200–220°C (400–425°F) for about 30 minutes. Serve hot on top of individual portions of Injera (page 71).

*Note:* You may choose to season each fish on greased aluminium foil then wrap it up and bake as above; the cooking time will be shorter, 15–20 minutes.

SERVES 4

# DORO WOT

## CHICKEN STEW

125 g (4 oz) butter or ghee

4 large onions, diced

185 g (6 oz) tomato paste

750 mL (1¼ pt) water

10 g (2 teaspoons) garlic salt

5 g (1 teaspoon) freshly ground black pepper

2 red chillies (hot peppers), finely diced or 2 teaspoons Berbere mix (page 70)

1 kg (2 lb) chicken pieces

6 hard-boiled eggs, shelled

'Wot' (pronounced 'whot') is the Ethiopian term for stew, and Doro Wot is chicken stew made in the Ethiopian style. It is delicious and thick and is generally served ceremoniously on the famous Ethiopian Injera Bread (page 71). Everyone digs into the Doro Wot and accompaniments, tearing off pieces of the bread to soak up even more of the Wot, which is eaten with the fingers.

You can substitute red meat for the chicken – the dish is then known as Beg Wot.

Melt butter or ghee in a heavy-based saucepan and sauté the onions for 10 minutes until golden. Mix the tomato paste with 125 mL (4 fl oz) water to form a creamy paste. Stir the paste into the onions with the garlic salt, black pepper, chillies (hot peppers) or Berbere, and the remaining 625 mL (¾ pt) water. Adjust seasoning and simmer gently on low heat for about 10 minutes.

Prick each chicken piece and each egg all over with a skewer or fork and add them to the simmering sauce. Stir well to ensure the chicken and eggs are well coated in sauce. Simmer on low heat for 30–40 minutes or until the chicken and eggs have absorbed the flavours of the sauce, the chicken is tender and the sauce has thickened.

Serve hot with Injera (page 71) or boiled rice. Set the dish of Injera as the centrepiece of the meal. Alternatively, do it the Ethiopian way: cover a large serving platter with Injera, place the Doro Wot in the centre surrounded by an assortment of vegetables and invite your guests to eat communally by breaking off pieces of Injera and scooping up the Doro Wot without using cutlery. It gives new meaning to intimacy!

SERVES 4

# KITFO

500 g (1 lb) lean, minced topside beef

1 onion, diced

60 mL (4 tablespoons) vegetable oil

Juice of 1 lemon, or 60 mL (4 tablespoons) wine or apple vinegar (optional)

10–20 mL (2–4 teaspoons) red chilli (hot pepper) sauce

Salt and lots of freshly grated black pepper to taste

5 g (1 teaspoon) each ground cumin, cinnamon, coriander (cilantro) and finely chopped garlic

An assortment of green salad vegetables, e.g. lettuce, alfalfa (lucerne), sunflower shoots, green capsicum (sweet or bell pepper) etc.

*Generally Africans prefer their meat well cooked (sometimes too well cooked), so this Ethiopian raw meat dish is quite unusual. In fact, it reminds me particularly of a Japanese recipe I was given years ago by a friend.*

*Ethiopians add a local yellow pepper called mitmita to the meat, believing that the hot pepper will kill any germs. Since this variety of pepper is not always available everywhere, I suggest using any variety of moist, coarsely grated prepared chilli (hot pepper) sauce.*

Put all the ingredients in a bowl and mix thoroughly together. Form into small balls or flat patties. Arrange salad on individual plates with the meat in the middle. Garnish as you wish and serve cold. It makes a light lunch.

*Note:* I have personally never been able to eat raw meat so I lightly cook my portion in the microwave for a few seconds then break up the meat with a fork and sprinkle it over my salad.

SERVES 4–6

---

# ETHIOPIA

An arid land of mountainous plateaux with serious erosion and drought problems, Ethiopia is also a country of great beauty and interest to the traveller prepared to work a bit harder to get off the beaten track. The intrepid traveller should look beyond the bureaucratic difficulties to the majesty of the rock hewn churches of Lalibela and the beautiful Rift Valley lakes, and perhaps sample transport by mule in one of the mountainous regions of this country now slowly opening up, having been previously cut off from the rest of the world for many years.

# ABISH

125 mL (4 fl oz) vegetable oil

1 large onion, diced

15 g (1 tablespoon) grated root ginger

15 g (1 tablespoon) finely chopped garlic

2 tomatoes, diced

500 g (1 lb) lean, minced beef

Salt to taste

2–3 eggs, beaten

15 g (1 tablespoon), turmeric

15 g (1 tablespoon), butter seasoned with 15 g (1 tablespoon) finely chopped parsley

Extra parsley for garnishing

250 g (8 oz) goat's cheese, grated (optional)

*Although the African tradition is to use meat as a flavouring or condiment and rarely as the main component of a meal, this simple dish uses meat as a stuffing for fruits and vegetables such as green, unripe pawpaw (papaya), green capsicums (sweet or bell peppers) or baked potatoes.*

*Ideally this dish should be cooked completely in butter, but because butter is expensive in much of Africa most people use just a tablespoon of it and season it with the herb of their choice.*

Heat the oil in a pan and sauté the onion until golden. Stir in the ginger, garlic, tomatoes, mince and salt. Cook on low heat for 15–20 minutes, stirring regularly to prevent burning. Combine the eggs with the mixture in the pan and cook for a further 10 minutes. Remove from the heat. Add the turmeric and seasoned butter and top with the parsley and cheese. Serve with rice or fresh bread; mix with steamed corn and eat by itself; or use it to stuff other vegetables.

SERVES 4

## THE CHOSEN ONES

A persistent belief in Ethiopia that Ethiopians are the chosen people of God stems from a long-held creation legend. According to this legend, God moulded the first humans from clay. He put the first batch into an oven to bake, but left them there too long and they emerged burnt and black, so he threw them away to the southern part of Africa. He took the second batch from the oven too soon and they were pasty and white, so he threw them northwards where they became the Arab and European populations. The third and final batch was just right and God put them in Ethiopia.

# SHIRO WOT
VEGETABLE STEW

500 mL (¾ pt) boiling water

250 g (½ lb) groundnut (peanut) paste (freshly ground from a health food shop)

60 g (4 tablespoons) butter

1 onion, diced

2 teaspoons Berbere mix (page 70) or 2-3 red chillies (hot peppers), diced

Salt to taste

250 g (½ lb) sweet corn (maize)

250 g (½ lb) root and green vegetables of your choice

250 g (8 oz) pumpkin or cabbage (optional)

1 big semi-ripe plantain or banana, cut into 6 rounds

15 g (1 tablespoon) tomato paste

*This particular wot or stew is very similar to the groundnut (peanut) stews from other parts of Africa, except that it is made with vegetables only. Shiro Wot is frequently used in Muslim areas of Ethiopia during periods of religious fasting such as Ramadan, when meat, dairy products and poultry are excluded from the diet. Meat, of course, can be added to Shiro Wot if you prefer.*

Blend together the boiling water and groundnut (peanut) paste, and set aside. Melt the butter in a large, heavy-based saucepan over low heat and sauté the onions and Berbere or chillies (hot peppers) for about 5 minutes. Stir in the blended groundnut (peanut) paste, season and simmer on low heat for about 30 minutes, stirring regularly to prevent sticking.

Add the rest of the ingredients and simmer for 15-20 minutes until the vegetables are cooked and the sauce has thickened. If using green vegetables, add them only in the last 5 minutes so they do not overcook. Serve with Injera (page 71), with rice or by itself.

SERVES 4

# EGGPLANT (AUBERGINE) AND BEAN SALAD

**3 large eggplants (aubergines), peeled and diced**

**Salt and pepper to taste**

**Juice of 1 lemon**

**60 mL (4 tablespoons) olive oil**

**2 cloves garlic, finely diced**

**500 g (1 lb) cold boiled beans of your choice**

**10 g (2 teaspoons) sugar**

*Eggplant (aubergine) is popular all over the north and north-eastern regions of Africa. It is a very versatile vegetable and can form the basis of dips and spreads, salads and stews.*

*Traditional African eggplants are cream-coloured and are smaller than their purple counterparts. Growing, they look just like clusters of eggs hanging on a low shrub. The cream and yellow varieties are commonest south of the Sahara.*

Place the eggplants (aubergines) in a bowl. Mix the salt and lemon juice together and pour over the eggplants (aubergines). Leave for 10–15 minutes.

Combine the oil, garlic, pepper and beans in a salad bowl with the eggplant (aubergine) and marinade. Toss the lot together well, sprinkle with the sugar and serve with hot bread.

SERVES 4

---

# BERBERE

Many Ethiopian dishes use the seasoning known as Berbere (pronounced 'bari baray') which is a combination of ground spices, pepper and salt. To make a western version of Berbere (in the absence of local Ethiopian spices):

Mix together 1 teaspoon each: ground cumin, ground coriander (cilantro), ground ginger, ground cardamom, ground fenugreek seeds, ground nutmeg, ground cinammon, ground cloves and onion powder.

Toast lightly in a heavy skillet or frying pan on low heat for 3–4 minutes, stirring constantly.

Next add: $\frac{1}{4}$ teaspoon allspice, 310 g (10 oz) cayenne pepper, 125 g (4 oz) paprika, 60 g (2 oz) salt and 30 g (1 oz) ground black pepper.

Continue toasting on low heat for approximately 10 minutes, stirring constantly. Remove from heat and cool. Store in an airtight container. It makes about 500 g (1 lb) and will last for about 1 year.

To make up a smaller quantity of a quick equivalent of Berbere:

Mix together 1 teaspoon ground ginger, $\frac{1}{2}$ teaspoon ground cinnamon, $\frac{1}{4}$ teaspoon ground dry mint and 90 g (3 tablespoons) cayenne pepper or paprika. Makes approximately 100 g (3 $\frac{1}{2}$ oz).

# INJERA

1 kg (2 lb) self-raising flour

250 g (½ lb) wholewheat plain flour

5 g (1 teaspoon) baking powder

500 mL (16 fl oz) soda water

*Injera is an Ethiopian flat bread – with a difference. This spongy, thin bread is generally made to dimensions large enough to cover a table, and it is, in fact, used in place of a cloth or table covering. Food such as Doro Wot (page 66) is then served directly onto the Injera for big communal meals.*

*Injera is usually made from Ethiopian-grown flour called 'teff' in the Armharic language. Teff is a cereal widely grown in Ethiopia for grain but in other countries as fodder. There are two kinds of teff: red (which is richer in iron and minerals) and white, and these account for the local differences in the colour of Injera.*

*It is often difficult to find teff flour in western shops, but there is a practical and easily made equivalent, which Lorna Harkrader came up with and which with permission from* The Africa News Cookbook *I have provided below.*

Combine the flours and baking powder in a bowl. Add the soda water, and mix to a smooth, thin batter.

Heat a large, nonstick skillet or frying pan. When a drop of water bounces on the pan's surface, it is ready. Tip enough batter from the bowl to cover the bottom of the pan, tilting the pan to coat the base evenly, then set it back on the heat. When the moisture has evaporated and small holes appear on the surface, remove the Injera. It should be cooked on only one side, and not browned.

If your first try is undercooked, you may need to cook it a little longer or make the next one thinner. As with French crêpes, be careful not to overcook or you will have a crisp bread which may be tasty but won't fold around servings of stew.

Stack the Injera one on top of the other as you cook, covering them with a cloth to prevent them drying out. To serve, lay the Injera on a platter or tray in overlapping concentric circles beginning with the inside and moving outwards until the edges of the outer ring fall over the edge.

SERVES 6–8

# KENYA

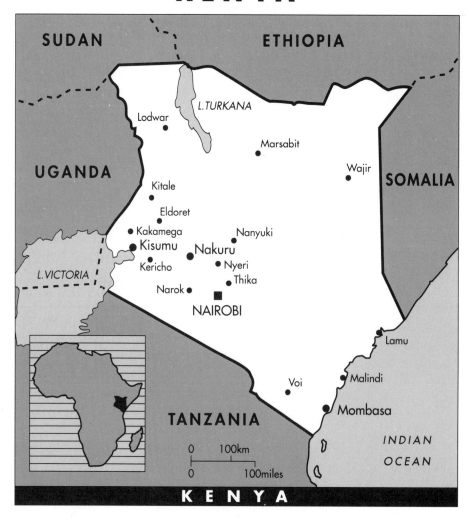

**Official title**  Republic of Kenya (known in Kiswahili as Djumhuri ya Kenya)

**Capital city**  Nairobi (means 'swamp')

**Official languages**  Kiswahili and English, although Kikuyu, Luo, Kikamba and Kiluhya are widely spoken

**Currency**  Kenya shilling (KS) = 100 cents

**Cash crops for export**  Tea, coffee, sugar, cotton, pyrethrum, wattle, sisal and pineapples

**Food crops**  Maize, sorghum, cassava, beans, vegetables, fruits, livestock and fish

**Total land area**  Approximately 582,600 sq km

# GIRIAMA GOURMET

**6 cloves garlic, chopped**

**1 onion, chopped**

**5 g (1 teaspoon) each saffron, cumin and turmeric**

**60 g (4 tablespoons) butter**

**2 kg (4 lb) fish fillets**

**Salt and pepper to taste**

**4 tomatoes, chopped**

**750 mL (1¼ pt) coconut milk**

*Giriama (pronounced 'ghe-ree-yah-mah') is a recipe given to me by my friend and colleague Mike Piper, an expatriate Kenyan, and his wife Jenny. It is a Kenyan coastal fish dish named after the Giriama people of Malindi. Flavoured with garlic, saffron, cumin, turmeric and coconut milk, it is a kind of regional fish curry.*

Stir-fry the garlic, onion and spices in butter for about 5 minutes. Stir in the fish pieces and salt to taste. Cook for about 10–15 minutes. Add the tomatoes and cook for a further 10 minutes. Stir in the coconut milk and simmer slowly for a further 15–20 minutes to reduce the sauce to a creamy texture.

To serve, the traditional recipe calls for a glowing piece of charcoal to be added before serving, as this is thought to put extra flavour and 'real' fire into the sauce. However, charcoal should only be used by professionals; it is not recommended for the average kitchen! It can be dangerous and also leaves small flakes of charcoal in the sauce.

SERVES 4 – 6

# CHICKEN IN COCONUT MILK

**Garlic salt to taste**

**125 mL (4 fl oz) vegetable oil**

**1 whole chicken, jointed into 6–8 pieces**

**3 medium onions, chopped**

**2 cloves garlic, chopped**

**4 large tomatoes, blanched, seeded and diced**

**Salt and pepper to taste**

**500 mL (¾ pt) coconut milk**

**1 bunch fresh coriander (cilantro)**

*There are a variety of coconut and meat dishes from countries surrounded by or bordered by the sea. But this particular chicken and coconut recipe from Kenya, with its overtones of mixed cultural influences, is special to me for its simplicity and because chicken is traditionally served in Africa on special occasions and to celebrate the presence of guests.*

*Chicken is not as commonplace in Africa as it is in industrialised countries. The birds are caught fresh from the backyard, plucked and prepared on the same day, lending a distinctive flavour to the dish.*

Rub the garlic salt and about 60 mL (4 tablespoons) oil all over the chicken pieces. Arrange on a charcoal grill and lightly brown or, alternatively, cook in the oven.

In a separate cooking pot, fry the onions and garlic in the remaining oil until they start to brown, then add the tomatoes and cook on a low heat for 5–10 minutes. Season to taste.

Combine the browned chicken pieces with coconut milk in a large saucepan and simmer for 5–10 minutes. Now combine the onion and tomato sauce with the chicken and coconut. Stir well, lower the heat and simmer slowly for 30–40 minutes until the coconut sauce reduces and the chicken becomes tender.

Pour the stew into a serving dish and top with fresh coriander (cilantro). Serve hot with boiled rice and vegetables of your choice.

SERVES 4 – 6

# SUKUMA WIKI
## LEFTOVERS STEW

250 g (½ lb) leftover meat, cooked or raw and chopped into bite-size pieces

90 mL (3 fl oz) vegetable oil

2 onions, diced

4 tomatoes, blanched, peeled and quartered

1 green capsicum (sweet or bell pepper)

Salt and black pepper to taste

500 g (1 lb) spinach (silver beet)

*This meat and vegetable recipe is another given to me by Mike and Jenny Piper. Mike, who has impeccable Swahili, told me that 'Sukuma Wiki' (pronounced 'su kuma wi-kee') is Kiswahili and literally translates as 'push the weak'. It is frequently served on the day before payday, when all that one might have in the kitchen are leftovers. I might add, however, that it is also available at most restaurants in Kenya — even at Nairobi's finest – on almost every day of the week!*

If you are using raw meat, start with this. Fry the meat lightly in a pan with hot oil. When the meat is nearly cooked, add the onions and continue cooking until they are soft and translucent. Add the tomato quarters with the green capsicum (sweet or bell pepper) and any other pre-cooked meat. Season with salt and pepper to taste and cook until the meat is done.

Stir in the chopped spinach (silver beet) and cook on a low heat for about 30 minutes, stirring periodically. Give the whole pan a final stir before serving with Ugali (page 87), boiled rice, plantain or bananas, or by itself.

SERVES 4

## RIFT VALLEYS AND SODA LAKES

The rift valleys of East Africa have formed along fault lines in the earth's crust. These valley are created by blocks of the crust dropping down, leaving surrounding areas of higher ground to form hills and mountain ranges. Mount Kenya and Mount Kilimanjaro (in Tanzania) are peaks created in such a way and both are actually extinct volcanoes.

Lakes form on the floors of the valleys, caused by run-off from the surrounding slopes. They are freqently shallow and have a high alkaline content created by a combination of high evaporation and volcanic minerals. Such lakes are called 'soda lakes'. Despite the high alkaline levels, many creatures exist in and around the lakes.

The main soda lakes in Kenya are Nakuru, Bogoria and Magadi; in Tanzania there is Lake Natron.

\* \* \*

## THE MAASAI

The Maasai, once a powerful and ferocious people, inhabit the open grasslands of the Rift Valley of Kenya. Ignoring the social and political changes that have taken place in that country, they have retained their nomadic ways, herding cattle, sheep and goats.

Cattle are of prime importance to the Maasai, for they believe that these beasts have been entrusted to them by the sky god Enkai. Their wealth and social status is measured by the number of cattle owned. In the arid areas of the Rift Valley, the livestock is moved seasonally, driven by the constant quest for water and grazing land.

As the cattle are of such significance, they are only slaughtered when they grow old, and then generally for ceremonial purposes, such as rites of passage. A mainstay of the Maasai diet is milk, which is carried in decorated gourds and may also be mixed with cows' blood. Any meat is provided from butchered goats and sheep.

It is also taboo to kill wild game except for buffalo and eland. The Maasai believe it is sacriligous to cultivate the land (and thus disturb the cattle fodder). Like the Ashantis, Mandingos, Fulanis (of West Africa) and the Zulus (of southern Africa), the Maasai are a very proud race. They regard Europeans as 'people of the paper' and disdain other groups who farm the land and adopt modern methods, calling them 'black Europeans'.

# IRIO

CORN (MAIZE) AND BEAN MASH

**250 g (8 oz) each beans or peas of your choice and lentils**

**Salt and pepper to taste**

**2 semi-ripe plantains or bananas, peeled and cut into 6 sections each**

**4 large potatoes, peeled and quartered**

**500 g (1 lb) corn (maize) kernels**

**60 g (4 tablespoons) butter**

*Although some Kenyans find this dish rather dull, I think it is wonderfully versatile. It is like a Kenyan version of 'Fuul Medames' (page 63). An innovative cook can make much of Irio, adding different flavourings such as garlic, fresh herbs and spices, and combining it with dried salted fish, seafood, minced meat; or stuffing it into various vegetables to bake.*

Soak the beans of your choice in cold water for two hours. Rinse them thoroughly under cold water. Put them in a large saucepan with water and salt. Bring to the boil and simmer for 15–20 minutes.

Add the lentils, plantains or bananas, potatoes, corn (maize) kernels and a little more water and salt if necessary. Bring to the boil and simmer slowly until all vegetables are soft and cooked. Drain off any excess water.

In a very large bowl, mash all the boiled vegetables and the butter together as smoothly as possible. At this stage, for variation, you can mash in any spice or herb seasoning, or any cooked fish or, meat, or even another vegetable such as pumpkin.

Serve by itself or as an addition to any meat or fish dish.

SERVES 4 – 6

# CRUNCHY N'DIZI
CRUNCHY BANANAS

8 bananas, peeled
125 g (4 oz) butter, melted
125 g (4 oz) groundnuts (peanuts) chopped

*This fruit combination recipe was supplied by my friends Mike and Jenny Piper. N'dizi (pronounced ndee-zi) is the Swahili word for 'bananas', and the crunchy groundnut (peanut) and banana pieces served with ripe Mango Fool (page 36) and ice-cream, or a sliver of unripe coconut, makes a delicious end to a meal.*

Steam the bananas in a large saucepan until heated through (a few seconds only). Be careful that they do not become too soft. Drain and roll in the melted butter. Now roll each one separately in chopped groundnuts (peanuts).

Arrange them on a baking dish and bake in the oven for 15 minutes at 190°C (375°F).

SERVES 4

## THE STRUGGLE FOR KENYA

Coastal Kenya was settled as early as the seventh century AD by Persian and Arab traders on the endless quest for ivory and slaves. The first Europeans to arrive were the Portuguese in the sixteenth century. They were constantly at war with the Arab population and their position was further weakened by the growth of English naval power in the Indian Ocean. The Portuguese were finally driven out of Kenya in the seventeenth century. The coastal area came under control of the Sultan of Oman and a flourishing trade in ivory and slaves was soon established.

East Africa is completely different from the arid wilderness, deserts or humid tropical forests of the north, central and western Africa. The region enjoys a peculiar tropical climate, which is dry and sunny. It favours the growth of exotic trees such as the African camphor, pencil cedar, baobab and podo, peculiar to the region.

# TANZANIA

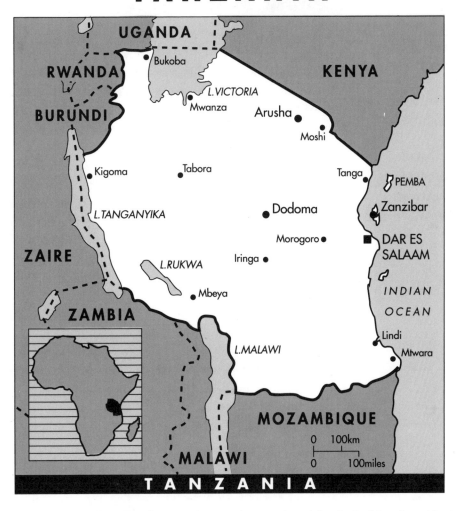

TANZANIA

**Official title**   United Republic of Tanzania (a union of Tanganyika and the islands of Zanzibar and Pemba)

**Capital city**   Dodoma (the former capital was Dar es-Salaam)

**Official languages**   Kiswahili and English

**Currency**   Tanzanian shilling (Tsh) = 100 senti

**Cash crops for export**   Tea, coffee, sugarcane, sisal, rubber, pyrethrum, cashew nuts. Spices and cloves from Zanzibar

**Food crops**   Maize, millet, sorghum, rice, cassava, groundnuts (peanuts), coconuts, yams, vegetables, plantains, bananas, livestock, poultry and fresh fish

**Total land area**   Approximately 945,000 sq km

# SUPUYA PAPAI

## PAWPAW (PAPAYA) SOUP

1 medium-large unripe pawpaw (papaya). It should feel firm when pressed

5 g (1 teaspoon) butter

1 large onion, finely chopped

500 mL (¾ pt) stock

Salt and pepper to taste

250 mL (8 fl oz) cream

1 teaspoon fresh, chopped chives

*Tanzanian food is not easy to describe: it may be easiest to classify as a local variation on Universal African food, with a strong tropical slant. With the much wider variety of fruits available in this country, recipes have been developed to use rather than waste them. This unusual but delicious soup made from pawpaw (papaya) is an example. It can be served hot or cold.*

Peel the pawpaw (papaya) and cut it into pieces. In a saucepan, heat the butter and fry the pawpaw (papaya) and onion without browning. Add the stock and seasoning and simmer until the pawpaw (papaya) is soft. Put the whole lot into a blender and blend until smooth. Add half the cream and mix in.

If serving cold, allow to stand in a cool place until cold then lightly pour on remainder of the cream and sprinkle the chopped chives on top before serving.

If serving hot after adding half the cream, return to the stove and heat on low. When hot, add the rest of the cream and the chives to decorate before serving.

SERVES 4–6

## THE SPICE ISLE

Most of mainland Tanzania consists of a plateau of which the Great Rift Valley is a dominant feature. To the north near the border with Kenya, is Mount Kilimanjaro, Africa's highest mountain, and on the border with Uganda, the largest lake in Africa, Lake Victoria. Offshore are several islands including Zanzibar, the Spice Island, and Pemba. Zanzibar has lured travellers to its exotic shores for centuries. Under the Arabs in the mid-nineteenth century, the island became the most important trade centre on the East African coast — supplying much of the world's cloves. It was also infamous for being the largest slaving entrepot of Africa's east coast.

**From Ethiopia** Beg Wot (Meat Stew) (page 66) and Injera Bread (page 71) with fresh vegetables

**From Tanzania**   A four-course banana meal (from left): Mtori with Coconut Cream
(Cream of Banana Soup) (page 81); Banana Fritters (page 88); Plantain Chips (page 88); sweet potatoes;
Ndizi ya na Nyama (Banana and Coconut Beef Stew) (page 84); and chilled Banana Wine (page 90)

**From Tanzania**    Mtori (Cream of Banana Soup) (page 81)

# MTORI

## CREAM OF BANANA OR PLANTAIN SOUP

**500 g (1 lb) lean beef, diced**

**2 large soup bones**

**1.5 L (2½ pt) cold water**

**Vegetable oil for frying**

**5 medium green bananas or plantains**

**1 medium onion, finely chopped**

**1 large ripe tomato, peeled and finely chopped**

**Salt and pepper to taste**

**5 g (1 teaspoon) butter**

*Pronounced 'm-tory', this Cream of Banana or Plantain Soup is a traditional dish from the Kilimanjaro region. It is very popular with nursing mothers, and while the men would traditionally consider it feminine to take liquid foods, an exception is made for this soup because it is so delicious! The excuse used is that the men are helping their wives to eat well!*

Put the meat and bones into a large saucepan with the water and bring to the boil. Simmer for 1 ½ hours to make a really strong stock.

Rub a little of the oil on your hands to prevent staining from the raw banana or plantain sap when you peel it. Peel and cut bananas or plantains into thin strips. Strain the stock and combine with the bananas or plantains, onion, tomato, salt and pepper. Simmer until all ingredients are very soft and cooked.

Mash with a whisk or blender to make a creamy soup. Add the butter to the soup and remove the soup bones. Re-heat (without boiling) and serve hot.

SERVES 4–6

# SAMAKI WA NAZI
COCONUT FISH CURRY

1 kg (2 lb) firm fish e.g. tuna, snapper, salmon or trevally

Salt to taste

45 mL (3 tablespoons) vegetable oil

1 medium onion, chopped

2 cloves garlic, crushed

15 g (1 tablespoon) curry powder

30 g (2 tablespoons) tomato paste

1–2 red chillies (hot peppers), (optional)

Juice of ½ lemon

500 mL (¾ pt) coconut milk

*This curry (prounced 'sah-ma-kih wah nahzi') is popular among the coastal dwellers of Tanzania and on Zanzibar, the 'Island of Spices'. With its location on the eastern coast of the African continent, Tanzania has been influenced by the cultures and cuisines of many other trading and seagoing nations, including India, Portugal and Persia (Iraq), so not all their recipes are strictly Tanzanian in origin. The results are a cuisine that is varied and exotic.*

Clean and rinse the fish, then season with salt. Heat the oil in a pan and brown the fish. Set aside and keep warm. In the same oil, fry onion until brown.

Add the garlic and stir; cook for 1 minute then add the curry powder, tomato paste, chillies (hot peppers), and lemon juice. Mix well and keep stirring so the mixture does not burn. Cook for 2–3 minutes.

Add the coconut milk and stir until it boils. Turn the heat down and add the fried fish. Simmer for about 10 minutes to allow the flavours to concentrate and the sauce to thicken to a creamy consistency. Serve hot with boiled or fried rice.

SERVES 4

# MCHICHA NA NYAMA
## BEEF AND SPINACH

45 mL (3 tablespoons) vegetable oil

1 large onion, finely chopped

500 g (1 lb) lean steak, cut into 5 cm (2 in) strips

5 g (1 teaspoon) root ginger, grated

Salt and pepper to taste

2 ripe tomatoes, peeled and finely chopped

1 green capsicum (sweet or bell pepper), finely chopped

1 big bunch of spinach (silver beet), stalks removed, leaves washed and chopped

*Mchicha is a staple green, rather like spinach (silver beet), which is eaten by everyone in Tanzania because it is cheap and easy to grow. Indeed, the more you harvest the small shoots, the more prolifically the plant grows. The plant can be found everywhere, including backyards, and as well as in this beef and spinach dish (pronounced 'mchi-cha-nah nyah-mah'), it can be used in soups, casseroles, salads, pies and with Ugali (page 87). If mchicha is unavailable, then spinach (silver beet) is a successful substitute.*

In a saucepan, heat the oil over medium heat and fry the onion without browning. Add the meat, ginger, salt and pepper and fry until the meat browns. Add the tomatoes and capsicum (sweet or bell pepper) and continue frying until the tomatoes are cooked and the meat is tender. Add the spinach (silver beet) and mix well. Serve immediately with Ugali (page 87).

SERVES 4

## THE LEGEND OF MOUNT KILIMANJARO

Mount Kilimanjaro has two peaks: one high and the other lower, with a serrated edge. Legend has it that many years ago the peaks were sisters. Kibo was the name of the taller one and Mawenzi was the smaller, although they were once the same height.

Mawenzi was very lazy and took care to visit her sister every day on the pretext of borrowing some hot coals or firewood. Invariably, however, she managed to linger not only for lunch but for dinner, too. After several years of feeding her sister twice a day, Kibo had had enough and, grabbing a traditional flat wooden spoon, hit Mawenzi several times on the head. To this day Mawenzi is shorter than her sister and has notches on her head — a testament to her laziness.

# N'DIZI YA NA NYAMA
### BANANAS OR PLANTAINS AND COCONUT BEEF STEW

1 kg (2 lb) lean beef, diced

250 mL (8 fl oz) water

Salt and pepper to taste

30 mL (2 tablespoons) vegetable oil

2 large onions, finely chopped

1 large ripe tomato, peeled and chopped

500 mL (¾ pt) coconut milk

5 firm, green bananas or plantains (must not be ripe)

250 g (8 oz) peas

*There are many African recipes that are based on bananas or plantains. This one, N'dizi ya na Nyama (pronounced ndee-zi yah nah n-yahmah'), is from the northern, western and southern regions of Tanzania where a variety of bananas are grown. In Africa plantains are a major produce and are preferred in cooking. Bananas can be substituted, particularly unripe ones (ripe bananas are rarely used). Plantains are larger and thicker than bananas and it is not advisable to eat them raw.*

In a saucepan, cook the meat with water and salt until tender. Set aside. Heat oil in a saucepan and fry the onions without browning. Add the tomato and meat mixture, adjust the seasoning to taste. Continue cooking until the tomatoes soften.

Add the coconut milk, stirring all the time until the mixture boils. Peel and cut the bananas or plantains into large pieces and add with the peas to the stew. Reduce heat and simmer for about 10–15 minutes or until the bananas or plantains are cooked but not mushy. Serve hot as a nutritious and filling stew.

SERVES 4–6

# MCHICHA NA NAZI
SPINACH (SILVER BEET) WITH COCONUT

1 large bunch of fresh
spinach (silver beet) or
500 g (1 lb) frozen spinach
(silver beet), thawed

250 mL (8 fl oz) coconut
milk

60 g (2 oz) ghee (Indian
cooking butter) or butter

1 onion, diced

1 tomato, diced

5 g (1 teaspoon) curry
powder

*Spinach is eaten widely all over Africa in a variety of forms: in combination with meat, fish, other vegetables or on its own with seasonings. Michicha Na Nazi is pronounced 'm-chi-cha nah nahzi' and is a kind of spinach from the small island of Lamu off the coast of Kenya.*

Remove the stalks and wash the fresh spinach (silver beet) thoroughly. Cook the fresh spinach (silver beet) in the coconut milk for about 5 minutes and drain well. Save the coconut milk.

In a saucepan, heat the ghee or butter and fry the onion, tomato and curry powder for about 5 minutes. Add the cooked spinach (silver beet) or the frozen spinach (thawed and drained) and the coconut milk. Stir all ingredients well and cook for a further 15 minutes over low heat. Serve hot with rice and fried fish dishes.

SERVES 4

## AFRICAN SPINACH

Many Africans refer to the leaves of local root vegetables as spinach, although they might be quite different from what Western cooks know as spinach or silver beet.

The triangular leaves of the cocoyam (taro) plant, known in the Ashanti language as 'kontomire', are called spinach in Ghana and other parts of West Africa. In Egypt, the local plant 'molohia' can be replaced with spinach or silver beet. In Tanzania, 'mchicha' a staple green leaf rather like silver beet, which grows prolifically, is also known locally as spinach.

The leaf of the cocoyam (taro) is popular across the Atlantic, too, in such countries as Trinidad. Known locally as 'dasheen', it is one of the varieties of plant that are generically called spinach.

'Spinach' is used in many recipes throughout Africa and wherever African cooking has spread. Don't worry if you are unable to find the local variety of plant because although the taste and texture may not be exactly the same, spinach or silver beet will do just as well.

# MBOGA YA MABOGA

PUMPKIN LEAVES AND FLOWERS IN CREAM

**500 g (1 lb) pumpkin leaves**

**8 pumpkin flowers, carefully washed**

**15 mL (1 tablespoon) vegetable oil**

**1 large onion, chopped**

**5 g (1 teaspoon) turmeric**

**1 red chilli (hot pepper), (optional)**

**1 large tomato, peeled and chopped**

**Salt to taste**

**60 mL (4 tablespoons) thickened (heavy or double) cream**

*Tanzanians are much more flexible in their use of ingredients, probably because of the influence of other cuisines. Not only do they frequently combine foods in ways unusual to the rest of the continent, but they use, for example, parts of plants which are not valued elsewhere. Hence this delicacy (pronounced 'mboh-gah ya ma-boh-gah') based on the pumpkin plant from central and southern Tanzania.*

Wash the pumpkin leaves and flowers and remove fibrous and spiky parts and stalks. Shred leaves finely and blanch in boiling salted water for 5 minutes then drain well and set aside.

Heat the oil in a saucepan and fry the onion until transparent but not brown. Add turmeric, chilli (hot pepper), tomato and salt. Reduce the heat and simmer on low, stirring frequently until the tomato is cooked.

Add the pumpkin leaves and cream and continue cooking on low heat for about 10 minutes. Stir in the pumpkin flowers and cook for a further 5 minutes.

Remove from heat and let the dish stand, covered, for 3–4 minutes. Remove the flowers from the stew and arrange them decoratively on top. Serve hot as an accompaniment to Ugali (page 87) and stew or rice and stew.

SERVES 4

# UGALI

1 L (1¾ pt) water or water and milk combined

60 g (2 oz) butter

Salt to taste (optional)

500 g (1 lb) corn (maize), millet, gari (coarse cassava powder) or sorghum flour

*Tanzania produces more corn (maize) than any other country in east Africa. Ugali is a stiff, steamed porridge usually made from maize and is a staple part of the diet, eaten by 90 per cent of the population. Since Ugali is inexpensive, poorer people can afford to combine it with mchicha (a variety of spinach or silver beet) sauces and be sure of one good meal a day. Ugali can be served hot or, after it has cooled, it can be fried, giving it a different texture.*

*Ugali is eaten all over east Africa and is known by different names in different regions: Mealie-meal in southern Africa; Sadza in Zimbabwe; and Banku in West Africa. Ugali may occasionally be made from gari (coarse cassava powder), millet or sorghum flour.*

Bring three-quarters of the water to the boil in a heavy-based saucepan which has a long handle for easier handling. Add the butter and salt. Put half the flour into a bowl, and add the remaining quarter of the water. Using a wooden spoon, stir together to form a smooth, thick paste. Set aside. When the water in the saucepan has boiled, pour in the thick paste and stir quickly and firmly for about a minute. Bring the mixture to the boil. Gradually add the remaining flour and mix, stirring all the time, until it thickens sufficiently to form a stiff dough. Caution – this stage requires a lot of wrist power and firm stirring.

The consistency can be varied according to taste by adding more or less flour and/or more water. When cooked, the Ugali should not stick to the sides of the pan. Serve hot with meat stew and/or vegetables. Ugali can be shaped into balls with an ice-cream scoop and served surrounded by the meat and vegetables.

SERVES 4

# PLANTAIN OR BANANA CHIPS

**2 semi-ripe plantains or bananas**
**Salt and pepper to taste**
**Vegetable oil for frying**

*Plantain or Banana Chips are a favourite of young and old alike. In Africa more Plantain Chips are eaten than potato chips!*

Peel the plantains or bananas and cut into very thin rings. Add salt and pepper to taste. Fry in very hot oil until crisp (not necessarily golden). Remove from the heat and drain on paper towels. Serve hot or cold with pre-dinner drinks.

# CHAPATI YA N'DIZI TAMU
## BANANA FRITTERS

**3 large, very ripe bananas**
**60 mL (4 tablespoons) milk**
**125 g (4 oz) caster sugar**
**30–60 g (2–4 tablespoons) cornflour (cornstarch)**
**5 g (1 teaspoon) ground nutmeg**
**Vegetable oil for shallow frying**

*Banana fritters vary in preparation styles around the world but this mashed variety (pronounced 'cha-pah-ti yah ndee-zi tah-mu') is different and fairly common in Africa.*

Peel the bananas, cut into halves, put in a mixing bowl and mash into a thick, coarse paste with your fingers, a wooden spoon or an electric blender.

Stir in all the ingredients except the oil and mix together thoroughly. You may need to add more or less cornflour (cornstarch) but the finished mixture should be thick and slightly coarse (which is why it is preferable to mash the bananas initially with your fingers).

Heat the oil in a skillet or frypan until just before the oil starts to smoke. Fry one tablespoon of the fritter mixture first as a test. If it burns immediately, the oil is too hot so reduce the heat. If it does not burn immediately but browns nicely, turn it over and cook the other side until both sides are golden and the fritter is firm.

Continue to fry the remaining mixture in small batches. Drain the fritters on paper napkins or on a wire sieve and keep them in a warm oven until all fritters have been cooked. Serve hot.

# CHILLED BANANA CREAM

*EGG CUSTARD*

**250 mL (8 fl oz) milk**

**2 eggs**

**30 g (2 tablespoons) caster sugar**

**2–3 drops vanilla essence**

*BANANA CREAM*

**Egg custard (above)**

**2 very ripe bananas, thoroughly mashed**

**15 g (1 tablespoon) sugar (optional)**

**250 mL (8 fl oz) whipped cream**

**3–4 drops food colouring of your choice**

*With so many Tanzanian recipes based on bananas or plantains, you could almost make an entire meal from these fruits! Cream of Banana Soup (page 81), and Banana and Coconut Beef Stew (page 84) could be followed by Chilled Banana Cream. Essentially this is a vanilla-egg custard which is mixed with whipped cream, sugar, mashed bananas and flavouring, and then frozen.*

*In the highlands and areas of Africa without refrigerators, desserts are covered and put outside in the cold night air. At daybreak they are gathered up, covered with cloth and kept in a cool, dark part of the house until it is time to serve.*

Heat the milk almost to boiling point (do not let it boil). Break the eggs into the hot milk, add the sugar and vanilla essence, and blend or whisk to a creamy mixture. Simmer slowly on very low heat, stirring continuously until it thickens into a smooth custard. Remove from the heat and put aside.

Mix together thoroughly the egg custard, mashed bananas and extra sugar. Blend in the whipped cream and the food colouring. Transfer into a serving dish and freeze. Decorate and serve with fresh banana cut into fancy shapes.

SERVES 4

# POMBE YA N'DIZI
PLANTAIN OR BANANA WINE

7 very ripe plantains or bananas, peeled and finely sliced

6 L (10 pt) water

2 kg (4 lb) sugar

4 x 2.5 (1 in) wide strips of soft toast

15 g (1 tablespoon) fresh yeast

*Yes, you can make a wine from plantains and bananas! This particular version is made with plantains and literally means 'alcohol with bananas.' The recipe is pronounced 'pom-bay yah ndee-zi'. It is delicious and can be drunk after three months. I prefer the process to take longer — up to six months — to allow the wine to mature and develop a stronger flavour.*

Boil the plantains or banana in the water for 20 minutes, strain and add the sugar to the liquid. Set aside to cool. Spread both sides of each strip of toast with fresh yeast and drop them into the strained liquid. Lightly cover the jar with a piece of muslin and store in a cool, safe place for 1 week. Strain the liquid after 1 week and store in an airtight container for 3 weeks, then open and strain for the third time. Store in an airtight container for a further 1 month.

Finally, open and strain for the fourth and last time, then bottle as wine and cork. The wine may now be chilled and served as normal, however, the longer it is left, the more mature it will become, so serve when it suits you. Personally, I prefer the total process to take 3–6 months.

MAKES 24–28 GLASSES

# ZIMBABWE

ZAMBIA

MOZAMBIQUE

R. ZAMBEZI

KARIBA DAM

L. KARIBA

Chinhoyi

HARARE

Chegutu

Marondera

Victoria
Falls

Kadoma

Hwange

Kwekwe

Mutare

Gweru

Masvingo

Bulawayo

Rutenga

BOTSWANA

Beitbridge

0    100km

0    100miles

R. LIMPOPO

ZIMBABWE

**Official title**   Republic of Zimbabwe

**Capital city**   Harare (the name of a former African ruler of the area, it means 'one who does not sleep')

**Official language**   English, although Shona and Ndebele are widely spoken

**Currency**   Zimbabwe dollar (Z$) = 100 cents

**Cash crops for export**   Maize, wheat, coffee,cotton, soya beans, groundnuts (peanuts) and tobacco

**Food crops**   Maize, wheat, soya beans, groundnuts (peanuts), cattle and fish farming

**Total land area**   Approximately 390,759 sq km

# HUKU NE DOVI

CHICKEN AND GROUNDNUT (PEANUT) STEW

1 whole, fresh 1.5 kg (3 lb) chicken

Salt to taste

125 mL (4 fl oz) vegetable oil

2 onions, diced

2 tomatoes, blanched and diced

250 g (½ lb) whole mushrooms

Dried vegetables, optional (page 93)

375 mL (13 fl oz) water

400 g (14 oz) freshly ground groundnut (peanut) butter

1 red chilli (hot pepper), optional

*Zimbabwe is a landlocked nation, so there is a greater emphasis on meat in the local cuisine in contrast to those other countries which have abundant supplies of ocean fish. Huku Ne Dovi (pronounced 'whoo-ku nay dorvi') is more frequently eaten for dinner than for lunch by the Shonas of Zimbabwe, and it is always accompanied by a carbohydrate dish such as rice or Sadza (page 97), a popular kind of dumpling made from millet flour.*

*In this part of the world chicken is generally considered to be a delicacy, and when it is served slightly 'tough' it confirms that your hosts have served you a proper 'professor' (free-range) chicken and not a processed one!*

Cut up the chicken into 8 individual pieces. Season with salt. In a saucepan, heat the oil and fry the chicken pieces and onions, turning until the chicken is evenly browned. Stir in the tomatoes and cook for about 3 minutes. Add the mushrooms and the dried vegetables. Stir well for 1 minute. Add the water and simmer slowly for approximately 30 minutes, until the chicken is more tender and nearly cooked.

Put the groundnut (peanut) butter into a bowl with enough boiling water to blend it into a smooth, runny paste. Add this paste and the chilli (hot pepper) when the chicken is tender and almost cooked. Mix in well and simmer on low heat, stirring regularly to avoid lumps and burning. Cook for about 20 minutes. When the sauce has thickened and the chicken is cooked, serve hot with rice or Sadza (page 97).

SERVES 8

# THE HOUSE OF STONE

The name Zimbabwe means 'House of Stone'. Lying between the Limpopo and Zambesi Rivers in the southern heart of Africa, Zimbabwe is more fortunate than many other African countries for it is self-sufficient in food.

Zimbabwe is the home of great stone ruins built over eight centuries ago by the Shona people, descendents of a culture that flourished during the Iron Age. The Shona still form the dominant racial group in the country, followed in number by the Ndebele.

Wonders of Zimbabwe include the Chinhoi Caves and the massive Victoria Falls, known as 'mosi oa tunya' or 'the smoke that thunders'.

\*　　\*　　\*

# WINTER VEGETABLES

Although Zimbabwe is fortunate in its capacity to be self-sufficient in food, its agriculture is still dependent on the seasonal variation in rainfall; the dry season during winter can lead to crippling drought. One method of dealing with this period of little growth is to dry various foods harvested after the rainy season.

Grains such as maize, millet, rice and sorghum can, of course, be stored in a variety of ways, but in Zimbabwe, as in other countries, vegetables harvested during summer and autumn are dried for later use in winter.

There are a number of vegetables treated in this manner in Zimbabwe. Some of them are:

*Bowara*　Pumpkin leaves, excluding the 'nhopi' variety. They can be eaten fresh or sun-dried for storage. The leaves are very soft and are frequently mixed with beef in stews, combined with the flesh of baby pumpkins and pumpkin flowers, or served with dovi (chicken).

*Derere*　This is the Zimbabwean name for okro (okra).

*Kovo*　A large-leafed vegetable the size of a cabbage, but bigger, sweeter and lighter in texture and taste. It too can be eaten fresh after harvest or stored for consumption during winter.

*Nyovhi*　A wild plant indigenous to Zimbabwe with small, narrow, green leaves. It is important to harvest the leaves at the right season or they will be bitter. Early nyovhi shoots usually herald the arrival of summer and the rainy season. Nyovhi is frequently eaten cooked and mixed with mushrooms and baby pumpkins, or in goat stew.

# NYAMA NE NYEMBA
### STEAK AND BEAN STEW

3 onions, thinly sliced

45 mL (3 tablespoons) vegetable cooking oil

1 kg (2 lb) shoulder steak or spareribs, diced

2 cloves garlic, crushed

1 green chilli (hot pepper), crushed

45 g (3 tablespoons) curry powder

2 medium tomatoes, sliced or diced

Salt and pepper to taste

1 kg (2 lb) cooked kidney beans

Juice of 1 lemon

*There seem to be innumerable varieties of beans, and they are an ever-present favourite of many 'soul food' menus. Apart from the protein and fibre content, beans are easy to grow and some varieties are hardy and drought-resistant, so they are a staple of the African diet all over the continent. Beans are versatile and delicious and can be eaten dried or fresh in a variety of dishes. Nyama Ne Nyemba is a Zimbabwean specialty.*

In a stew pot, brown the onions in the oil until golden brown. Add the meat and sauté over medium heat for about 5 minutes, stirring continuously. Lower the heat and cook gently for a further 15–20 minutes. Add the garlic, chilli (hot pepper) and curry powder and cook for about 3 minutes. Stir in the tomatoes and cook for another 3 minutes.

Season to taste, stir in the cooked beans and simmer over low heat for about 15 minutes.

Transfer to a serving dish and drizzle the lemon juice all over the top. Garnish as you wish and serve with boiled rice, Sadza dumpling (page 97) or simply by itself as a nutritious meal.

SERVES 4–6

# MAHOBHO or SADZA NDIURAYE
SPICY MEAT AND VEGETABLE STEW

## SAUCE

**30 mL (2 tablespoons) vegetable oil**

**½ cabbage, thinly sliced**

**1 turnip, peeled and diced**

**1 large onion, diced**

**2 green chillies (hot peppers), thinly sliced**

**2 large tomatoes, blanched, peeled and diced**

**15 mL (1 tablespoon) honey**

**375 mL (12 fl oz) hot water**

**Salt and pepper to taste**

## MEAT

**30 mL (2 tablespoons) vegetable oil**

**1.5 kg (3 lb) lean stewing steak, diced**

**1 large onion, diced**

**2 potatoes, roughly diced**

*Mahobho means 'plenty', while this dish's alternative name, Sadza Ndiuraye (because the dish is always served with Sadza dumpling), translates as 'Sadza don't kill me'! A Zimbabwean friend of mine, Gus, swears this recipe makes a wonderful hangover cure. I suppose this could be where the name 'Sadza don't kill me' comes from: the dish is designed to kill or cure you quickly — whichever way, it will put you out of your misery!*

Prepare the sauce first. In a large pan heat the oil and lightly fry the cabbage, turnip, onion, and the green chillies for about 3–4 minutes. Stir in the tomatoes and cook until they are soft. Mix the honey and hot water and add to the vegetables, with salt and pepper. Simmer for approximately 10 minutes or until the vegetables are soft and cooked (cook for less time if you prefer crunchier vegetables). Set aside to add to the meat.

To cook the meat, heat the oil in a pan over medium heat, and sauté the steak and the onion for 5 minutes. Add the potatoes and stir for a further 5 minutes. Add the prepared sauce. Cook for about 10 minutes over low heat, stirring occasionally. Serve hot with Sadza (page 97) when meat and vegetables are cooked and tender.

SERVES 4–6

## ZIMBABWEAN SAYING

'Hunge rakatsigir wa nemuto': 'For Sadza to enter it must be supported by the sauce — always!'

# NHOPI DOVI
## PUMPKIN WITH GROUNDNUT (PEANUT) SAUCE

**1 medium mashamba, or, as an alternative, butternut pumpkin peeled, seeded and diced**

**500mL (¾ pt) water**

**500g (1 lb) groundnut (peanut) paste**

**Salt or sugar to taste**

*A mashamba is a Zimbabwaen variety of pumpkin which bears an uncanny resemblance to a melon and has green flesh. Nhopi Dovi is a Shona recipe; the Ndebele people have a similar recipe which uses a different pumpkin called Mbaqanga. It has yellow flesh and creates a much thicker dish. Both recipes are very popular with children.*

Boil the mashamba or pumpkin in the water until cooked thoroughly. It should be very soft, ready to mash. Drain away excess water. Stir in the groundnut (peanut) paste. Mash both thoroughly to form a creamy, smooth paste.

Depending on your taste, add sugar or salt to make it sweet or savoury. Serve hot or cold as a lunch. When cold, it sets to a jelly-like mass.

SERVES 4

---

## THE LEGEND OF THE FIG TREE

A man of Zimbabwe searched every day for food for his family. As well, he would work on other people's land to earn what money he could. As food was so scarce he preferred to sleep under a tree during his midday break. Sleep generally brought him peace, but one day his hunger woke him up. In desperation he sang 'Somebody feed me; please feed me before I die'. And a miracle occurred! The fig tree under which he had been sleeping suddenly grew fruit which dropped around him. With joy he ate his fill but selfishly did not take home any of the fruit for his family. That evening he was too full to eat his meal.

He told no-one about the miracle tree but returned every day to sing to and gorge himself on fruit. And every day he returned home too full to eat with his family. At first they were concerned, but seeing he remained healthy, his children grew suspicious and secretly followed him. They saw what happened and decided to teach their father a lesson. The next day, before he arrived the children sang to the tree and gathered the fruit as it fell. Then they climbed the tree to wait.

When their father arrived he began to sing to the tree but instead of the fruit he was pelted with stones. That night he ate his Sadza in silence!

**From Nigeria**   Gari Foto (page 103) with a green melon drink

**From Nigeria** Chin Chin (Sweet Dough Balls) (page 105) and Nigerian Sweet Puffs (page 106)

**From Jamaica and Ghana** Jerk Pork (page 135) with Chilli Sambal (page 22)

**From Jamaica**   Sweet Potato Pone (page 137)

# SADZA DUMPLING

2.5 L (3¾ pt) water

1 kg (2 lb) mealie-meal (white maize flour) or rapoko (red millet flour) or ordinary millet flour

*Due to its enormous popularity, Sadza is regarded as Zimbabwe's national dish. Like the West African Banku, the East African Ugali, the Zambian Ntsima and the South African Mealie-meal, Sadza is a stiff, steamed dumpling made from white maize flour or rapoko (red millet flour) and served with stews or roasted meat, fish or vegetables and sauce.*

Bring 1.5 L (2¼ pt) of the water to the boil in a heavy-based saucepan with a long handle for easy handling. Mix half the mealie-meal with the remaining cold water to form a smooth paste. Add this paste to the boiling water, stirring vigorously to avoid lumps, until it boils again. Cover and continue to boil for 5 minutes.

Gradually add the remaining mealie-meal, one-quarter at a time, stirring thoroughly and firmly until the whole mixture thickens. You need a firm wrist — as the mixture thickens, the porridge gets firmer and more difficult to stir. Reduce the heat, cover the pan and cook for another 3 minutes.

Wet a small bowl with cold water and use the wet bowl to form the mixture into individual portions. Alternatively, you can serve the Sadza as one large family meal. Serve hot with vegetables and stew or roast meat or fish with the gravy of your choice.

SERVES 4

# NIGERIA

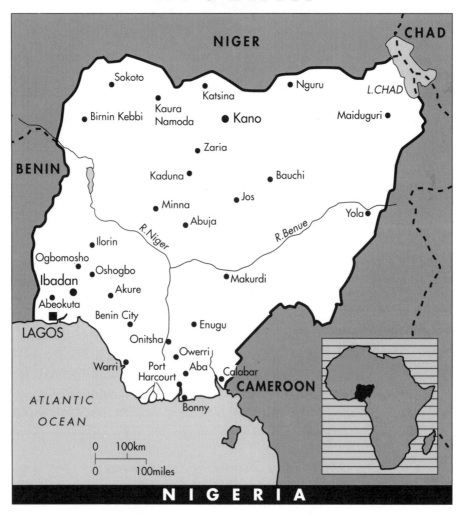

NIGER
CHAD
Sokoto
Katsina
Nguru
L.CHAD
Kaura
Namoda
Kano
Maiduguri
Birnin Kebbi
BENIN
Zaria
Kaduna
Bauchi
Minna
Jos
Abuja
R.Niger
R.Benue
Yola
Ilorin
Ogbomosho
Oshogbo
Makurdi
Ibadan
Akure
Abeokuta
Benin City
Enugu
LAGOS
Onitsha
Owerri
Warri
Port
Harcourt
Aba
Calabar
CAMEROON
ATLANTIC
OCEAN
Bonny
0    100km
0    100miles
NIGERIA

**Official title**   Federal Republic of Nigeria

**Capital city**   Abuja (new federal capital) (Lagos/former capital – main port)

**Official language**   English, although Hausa, Yoruba and Igbo are widely spoken

**Currency**   Naira (N) = 100 kobo

**Cash crops for export**   Cocoa, coffee, cotton, rubber, palm oil, palm kernel, livestock and poultry

**Food crops**   Sorghum, maize, rice, millet, wheat, yams and groundnuts (peanuts)

**Total land area**   Approximately 924,000 sq km

# OKRO (OKRA) SOUP

500 g (1 lb) lean topside beef, (see Note)

60 mL (4 tablespoons) vegetable oil

3 medium onions, finely chopped

3 large ripe tomatoes, blanched, peeled and puréed

500g (1 lb) fresh okro (okra), topped and tailed and sliced into thin rounds

2 red chillies (hot peppers), finely chopped, or chilli powder to taste

15 g (½ oz) salted beef

10 g (2 teaspoons) tomato paste

1 L (1¾ pt) water

A small piece of 'kaawé' or local meat tenderising stone (optional)

15 g (1 tablespoon) dried, ground prawns (shrimp)

6 large green prawns (shrimp), peeled

125 g (4 oz) crayfish meat

½–1 kg (1–2 lb) smoked fish (preferably few

*This is a dish that is native to Nigeria. Based on meat, smoked fish, seafood and vegetables, including, of course, okro (okra), I'm convinced that, along with the Ghanaian Okro Stew, it forms the basis of the now world-famous 'gumbo' of New Orleans and the Caribbean.*

Remove fat and sinew from the meat and cut into chunks 6-8 cm (2½–3in). Leave meat on the bone. Put all the meat in a large saucepan and add the oil, a quarter of the onions, a quarter of the tomatoes, a quarter of the okro (okra), a quarter of the chillies (hot peppers) and the salted beef. Sauté for about 10 minutes, stirring all the time until the meat is 'sealed' on the outside.

Blend the rest of the onions, tomatoes, chillies (hot peppers), chilli powder and the tomato paste with all the water and add it to the meat mix with the 'kaawé'. Bring to the boil, lower the heat and simmer for about 10 minutes. Add the rest of the okro (okra) and simmer for a further 20 minutes. Check to see if the meat is tender.

Add the dried, ground prawns (shrimp), the green prawns (shrimp), the crayfish meat and the smoked fish and continue to simmer for 10–15 minutes. Adjust salt to taste and continue simmering on low heat until the volume of water is reduced and the meat is tender. You may need to actually add more water to help the meat cook until tender, depending on the sort of meat chosen. When all the ingredients are cooked, the soup should be creamy and chunky, with the flavours of okro (okra), crayfish and meat vying for attention. Serve hot with Fufu (page 13), Semolina Dumpling (page 24), Eba (page 103) or rice.

*Note:* You can also use lamb chops, cutlets, skirt beef and cubes of salted beef. Four pieces of salted, boiled pigs' trotters make the dish taste delicious.

SERVES 6

# THE AFRICAN LIFELINE

Nigeria took its name from the River Niger, which is an important lifeline not only to Nigeria but to the other African countries through which it flows: Sierra Leone, where the river rises, Guinea, Mali and Niger.

Like many coastal West African countries, Nigeria suffered under the slave trade of the seventeenth and eighteenth centuries when the Portuguese, British and other European nations established slave-trading stations in the rich delta of the Niger, the largest in Africa. These coastal stations served as collection points and embarkation stations for the slave ships journeying across the Atlantic to the Americas and West Indies.

Nigeria has such a variety of people and cultures making up its population of 90 million people that it is impossible to pick a national dish.

Each area has its own regional favourite depending upon tradition, custom, religion and availability of food. Available food varies according to the season: the 'hungry season' is before the rains arrive in March to May; while the 'season of surplus' follows the harvest in October and November.

The northern (and mostly Muslim) peoples have diets based on beans, sorghum and brown rice; the eastern, largely Ibo-speaking people, eat gari (coarse cassava powder) dumplings and yams; the people in the south-east largely prefer a seafood and yam stew; while the mainly Yoruba people in the south-west eat gari with local varieties of spinach and okro (okra) in stews or soups.

Urban dwellers tend to buy their food on the streets from 'chop bars', street stalls, hawkers or from restaurants. The most popular foods are dishes based on cassava, yams, okro (okra), beans, plantains or skewered meat dishes.

# WHITEBAIT AND PEPPER SAUCE

1 kg (2 lb) whitebait or sprats

10 g (2 teaspoons) garlic salt

15 g (1 tablespoon) paprika

15 g (1 tablespoon) cornflour (cornstarch)

15 g (1 tablespoon) freshly grated root ginger

Vegetable oil for deep-frying

*PEPPER SAUCE*

2 large onions, finely chopped

4 cloves garlic, finely diced

Root ginger, grated

10 red chillies (hot peppers), finely chopped

4 large tomatoes, finely diced

Salt to taste

10 g (2 teaspoons) shrimp paste or 125 g (4 oz) powdered shrimp

*Like many West Africans, the inhabitants of Nigeria are big fish-eaters. Whitebait is a favourite and this particular recipe blends the crunchy and delicious little fish with a piquant sauce. Although it can be eaten as a main course with cornmeal dumplings (page 24), vegetables and rice, in Africa it is most frequently served as an accompaniment to drinks.*

Wash the fish and dry with paper towels. Place in a bowl with garlic salt, paprika, cornflour (cornstarch) and half the grated ginger. Mix well making sure the fish is well coated.

Heat the oil in a deep frypan or heavy-based saucepan and deep-fry the fish in batches. Remove each batch as the fish becomes crispy and firm (fish must be crisp and crunchy but be careful not to burn it). When the fish is cooked and ready, drain in a wire sieve lined with paper towels. Set aside and keep warm.

To make the sauce, fry the onions, garlic, chillies (hot peppers) and the remaining ginger in approximately 30 mL (2 tablespoons) of the oil used to fry the fish. Fry until light brown. Add the tomatoes and salt. Stir well and cook for approximately 10 minutes. Finally, stir in the shrimp paste or powder and simmer for an extra 1–2 minutes.

Remove from the heat and serve in small bowls or plates placed in the middle of a larger bowl or plate which is filled with the crunchy fried fish. The sauce is served as a dipping sauce for the fish and can be accompanied by side dishes of rice or root vegetables or crudités of carrot, mushroom, cauliflower or zucchini (courgette).

*Note:* Quantities of chillies (hot peppers) and tomatoes may be altered to taste.

SERVES 4

# NIGERIAN BEEF STEW

500 g (1 lb) good quality, lean beef, in large chunks

10–20 g (2–4 teaspoons) chilli powder

60 g (4 tablespoons) cornflour (cornstarch)

Salt to taste

180 mL (6 fl oz) vegetable oil

4 medium onions, cut in thin, semi-circular strips

4 large tomatoes, blanched, peeled and puréed

500 mL (¾ pt) water

2 g (4 teaspoons) tomato paste

*Unlike those of some European countries, very few African dishes are based solely on meat since it does not form a staple part of the traditional African diet. From amongst the many dishes native to Nigeria, however, this is a traditional meat dish. It is very hard to go past this rich Yoruba stew! (The Yoruba is one of the major traditional groups of south-western Nigeria.)*

Season the meat with half the chilli powder, half the cornflour (cornstarch) and some salt. Heat the oil in a heavy-based saucepan and sauté the meat until browned. Remove the meat and set aside in a large bowl. Pour off the oil and save. Do not wash the saucepan. Add a small amount of water to cover just the base of the saucepan and bring to the boil on low heat. The boiling water will blend with the meat juices from the base of the pan. Remove from the heat and add this juice to the fried meat.

Now clean the saucepan and pour in the oil used to fry the meat. Blend in the rest of the cornflour (cornstarch) and gently heat. When the flour starts to brown, add the onions and sauté until browned. Quickly stir in the puréed tomatoes. Combine the water with the tomato paste and stir in. Return the meat and juices to the pan and stir well. Taste the stew and adjust the seasoning to your taste. Simmer slowly for 10 minutes or until meat is tender and sauce thickened. Serve with hot, boiled, long-grain white rice. Skim off any excess oil before serving.

SERVES 4

# GARI FOTO

125 mL (4 fl oz) vegetable oil

3 medium onions, finely chopped

2 red chillies (hot peppers), finely chopped (optional)

4 ripe tomatoes, blanched, peeled and finely diced

15 g (1 tablespoon) tomato paste

125 mL (4 fl oz) water

Salt and pepper to taste

375 g (¾ lb) gari (coarse cassava powder)

1 egg, scrambled in oil without milk

1 lettuce and 2 extra tomatoes to garnish

*This recipe, pronounced 'gahri fortor', is based on the wonderful and versatile staple root vegetable of the African diet — gari (coarse cassava powder). Gari Foto is a kind of risotto based on gari instead of rice. It looks like a Jollof (an African risotto) and could even be called Gari Jollof. Like rice, gari (coarse cassava powder) is the basis of many dishes; it is economical and high in fibre. And, again like rice, it can swell to twice the amount in water!*

*Gari Foto can be served at breakfast but also as part of a main course at dinner! It has travelled across the world and is commonly eaten in Brazil (as farinhe de mandioca), and parts of the West Indies such as Tobago.*

In a heavy-based large saucepan, heat the oil and fry the onions with the chillies (hot peppers) until the onions are light brown.

Stir in the diced tomatoes and cook for 2 minutes. Add the tomato paste, the water and salt and pepper to taste. Simmer for 4–5 minutes, stirring constantly to prevent burning.

Put the gari (coarse cassava powder) in a bowl. Add an equal amount of cold salted water to the gari (coarse cassava powder) and stand for 10–15 minutes until the gari (coarse cassava) swells. Fluff out the gari (coarse cassava powder) with a fork then add it, with the scrambled egg, to the onion and tomato sauce. Stir well to blend so the mixture looks pink. Now the Gari Foto is ready.

Serve on lettuce leaves, garnish with slices or fancy-cut tomatoes and serve.

EBA (NIGERIAN VARIATION)
Combine 375 g (10 oz) gari with a pinch of salt and 500 mL (16 fl oz) of boiling water. Gari should absorb most of the water, but drain off any excess water if necessary and quickly knead into a firm, soft, smooth dough with a wooden spoon. Form into rounds and serve hot with stews and soups.

SERVES 4

# MOI-MOI WITH GREEN VEGETABLES

250 g (½ lb) black-eyed beans

500 mL (¾ pt) cold water

1 medium onion, brown or white, finely chopped

30 mL (2 tablespoons) vegetable oil

30 g (2 tablespoons) tomato paste

1 egg

Salt and pepper to taste

Parsley or fresh vegetables to garnish

*Although the name might appear French, Moi-moi is wholly Nigerian — and is pronounced 'moy-moy'. There are many variations on this savoury pâté, which uses one of Africa's stable foods, beans, this time of the black-eyed variety. It is not only delicious but has a wonderful contrasting texture of coarseness and smoothness. Serve it with a variety of fresh vegetables and it makes a perfect light lunch or appetiser before dinner.*

Soak the black-eyed beans in water overnight. Rinse and place in a saucepan with the cold water and a pinch of salt. Boil until the beans are nearly tender. Check regularly to ensure the pan does not boil dry. Drain all the water and cool the beans for about 20 minutes.

Place the boiled beans, onion, oil, tomato paste, egg and salt to taste in a blender or food processor. Blend until thick and semi-smooth.

Pour into a greased steamer or microwave dish and cook until firm to the touch and coming away from the sides of the dish. If using a steamer, place over hot water for 25–30 minutes. Insert a skewer to check if the middle is cooked; if not, cook for a little longer. If you prefer to use a microwave use a medium setting for 15–25 minutes.

Remove from the heat and cool for 10–15 minutes. Place a plate over the top of the dish and tip the pâté onto the plate. Serve, garnished with fresh lettuce, mushrooms, tomatoes and parsley or other ingredients of your choice.

SERVES 4

# CHINCHIN

125 g (4 oz) self-raising flour

125 g (4 oz) plain flour

5 g (1 teaspoon) baking powder

125 g (4 oz) caster sugar, or more, to taste

5 g (1 teaspoon) grated nutmeg

10 g (2 teaspoons) dried yeast

125-180 mL (4-6 fl oz) water mixed with food colouring (optional)

Vegetable oil for deep-frying

*These small, round, sweet West African dough balls are particularly popular at festive occasions such as weddings, christenings, birthdays and at Christmas. In Ghana they are called 'Toogbei' (the name of a dish frequently changes from country to country in Africa).*

*The literal translation of Toogbei is 'sheep's balls' and, as they can be brightly coloured on the inside with food colouring, we referred to them when we were children as 'the crown jewels'!*

*There is a variation to the basic recipe: by adding milk and eggs the dough becomes much richer.*

Sift the flours and the baking powder together in a mixing bowl. Add the sugar, nutmeg and yeast and mix in. Make a well in the centre and stir in enough water and colouring to make a dough. Add small amounts of water at a time so the dough is not too hard and not too soft. Cover and stand for 1 hour to swell.

Using your cupped fingers, scoop up small amounts of the dough to form small balls. Gently drop the balls of dough into hot oil to deep-fry. The outside browns quickly; lower the heat immediately the outside browns, so the centre can cook more slowly. Turn over to brown both sides. When cooked, remove from the heat and drain on paper towels. Serve hot or cold with other party foods and drink.

*Note:* The same dough can be used to fry bigger dough balls but they are not considered as special for parties!

SERVES 4–6

# NIGERIAN SWEET PUFFS

## RUBBING METHOD

**500 g (1 lb) plain flour**

**5 g (1 teaspoon) baking powder**

**Salt to taste**

**60 g (2 oz) butter**

**60 g (2 oz) caster sugar**

**2.5 g (½ teaspoon) grated nutmeg**

**½ beaten egg**

**180 mL (6 fl oz) half milk/half water**

**Vegetable oil for deep-frying**

## CREAMING METHOD

**60 g (2 oz) butter**

**125 g (4 oz) caster sugar**

**1 egg**

**60 mL (2 fl oz) diluted milk (30 mL/1 fl oz water and 30 mL/1 fl oz milk)**

**2.5 g (½ teaspoon) grated nutmeg**

**Flavouring essence of your choice e.g. vanilla, banana, coconut or rum**

**Salt to taste**

**5 g (1 teaspoon) baking powder**

**60 g (2 oz) plain flour**

**Vegetable oil for deep-frying**

*The sweet, fried shortcrust pastry made in this recipe can be twisted into a variety of decorative shapes to be served as a treat on special occasions, particularly at Christmas. The puffs are common throughout West Africa and, like many traditional African dishes, have spread to the West Indies.*

*There are two methods for making the pastry: the rubbing method and the creaming method.*

In a bowl sift the flour, baking powder and salt together and rub in the butter. Add the sugar and nutmeg and make a well in the centre.

Blend the egg and the milk-water mixture together. Pour into the centre of the flour and butter and mix well by hand to form a pastry dough. On a lightly floured chopping board, roll out the pastry to an even thickness. Cut into 5 cm (2 in) diamond shapes and cut a slit in the middle of each diamond. Pull one diagonal end through the centre slit.

Heat oil to very hot and fry the pieces of twisted pastry until brown and cooked (try one first). Drain off excess oil on paper towels and serve hot or cold.

SERVES 4

In a bowl cream the butter and sugar together. Blend in the egg. Add the diluted milk, nutmeg and flavouring essence of your choice. Set aside.

In another bowl, sift the salt, baking powder and flour together. Add the egg and milk mix to form a firm dough. Roll out on a floured board and proceed as with the rubbing in method.

SERVES 4

# BRAZIL

**Official title**   Federative Republic of Brazil

**Capital city**   Brasilia

**Official language**   Portuguese, although English and French are spoken in business

**Currency**   Cruzeiros (Cr $) = 100 centavos

**Cash crops for export**   Coffee, sugar, tobacco, cotton, sisal, rubber, jute, coroa fibre, cassava, soya beans, cocoa beans, castor beans, bananas, oranges, carnauba wax and nuts

**Food crops**   Maize, wheat, rice, sugar, soya beans, groundnuts (peanuts), some fruit, vegetables, livestock and fish

**Total land area**   Approximately 8,512,000 sq km

# CARURÚ

1 kg (2 lb) green prawns (shrimp)

Olive oil for frying

2 cloves garlic, diced

2 onions, grated

4 tomatoes, chopped

1 capsicum (sweet or bell pepper), diced

400 mL ($^2/_3$ pt) coconut milk

500 g (1 lb) dried prawns (shrimp)

2 tablespoons dênde (palm) oil, to taste

1 kg (2 lb) okro (okra), cut in 2.5 cm (1 in) pieces

Green chillies (hot peppers) to taste, chopped

*This Brazilian dish is so similar in many ways to Ghanaian Okro (Okra) Stew that I feel sure that it is one of those recipes carried west from Africa during the slave trade and then modified over generations to suit the new local conditions.*

Wash and peel the prawns (shrimp) in a bowl of warm water; reserve this water. In a frying pan, heat the olive oil and gently fry the garlic, onions, tomatoes and capsicum (sweet or bell pepper). Add the prawns (shrimp) and cook for 10 minutes. Add the coconut milk, dried prawns (shrimp), and the dênde (palm) oil. Continue cooking for 10–15 minutes.

Cook the okro (okra) in the reserved prawn (shrimp) water. When cooked, drain, and mix the okro (okra) with the prawn (shrimp) mixture. Heat gently. Add the chopped chillies (hot peppers) to taste and serve with boiled rice.

SERVES 4

---

## BAHIA

Bahia is the region on the north-east coast of Brazil which still maintains strong cultural ties to West Africa, particularly Nigeria.

Discovered in 1501 by early Portuguese explorers, the region was originally called Bahia de Todos os Santos, or All Saints Bay. Like the British, the Portuguese brought in indentured slave labour from Africa to build their colonies in South America, as well as using the local Amerindian peoples.

The cultures have co-existed in compromise ever since, maintaining certain separate cultural and religious activities, but blending in the necessities of day-to-day life.

# BOBO OF PRAWNS (SHRIMP)

**1 kg (2 lb) cassava, peeled, washed and diced**

**500 mL (¾ pt) coconut milk mixed with ½ teaspoon salt**

**60 mL (4 tablespoons) olive oil**

**2 onions, diced**

**4 tomatoes, chopped**

**1 clove garlic, diced**

**1 bunch fresh coriander (cilantro), washed and chopped**

**1 kg (2 lb) green prawns (shrimp)**

**30 mL (2 tablespoons) dênde (palm) oil**

**Whole red chillies (hot peppers) to taste**

**Salt to taste**

*This is a most unusual way to cook prawns (shrimp). The dênde (palm) oil and cassava signal that the recipe is of African origin but the method shows a Portuguese influence – a blend of two cultures to create a unique flavour.*

Boil the cassava in a small amount of water flavoured with 30–45 mL (2–3 tablespoons) of the salted coconut milk until cooked. Divide the cassava into two and put one half through a blender or food processor.

In a frying pan, heat the olive oil and sauté the onions, tomatoes, garlic and coriander for about 5 minutes. Add the prawns (shrimp) and gently simmer for 5–7 minutes.

Add the blended cassava, the diced cassava, the remaining coconut milk, dênde (palm) oil and the chillies (hot peppers) and salt to taste. Serve with steamed rice.

*Note:* If you have difficulty buying dênde (palm) oil, use another vegetable oil and add 15 g (1 tablespoon) turmeric to it.

SERVES 4–6

# INVOKING THE SPIRITS

It is perhaps in worship and related dance and music that the African influence on Brazil appears most striking. The strong Nigerian origins can be traced through the continued worship in both name and practice of Ogun, Obatala, Shango and other Nigerian tribal gods.

While most slaves were forced to convert to Christianity, a number or original beliefs and customs were preserved as a means of keeping in touch with the ancestral homeland and maintaining cultural identity.

Although some customs survived intact, others became mixed with elements of Christian belief and evolved into forms of worship that became distinctive in particular regions: thus candomble, macumba and unganda in Brazil; shango in Trinidad; santeria in Cuba; and voodoo in Haiti. So, contrary to popular belief, voodoo is not an African form of witchcraft but a hybrid form of worship.

All the religions, however, do involve some form of ritualistic African-style drum music to invoke the spirits' participation. The ceremonies often culminate in trance-like dancing during which the followers are apparently possessed by the deity. Frequently the 'possessed' dance until they collapse with exhaustion.

It is said that the Brazilian samba and the Cuban rumba have their origins in these dances.

# VATAPA

Olive oil for frying

1 whole 2 kg (5 lb) chicken cut in pieces and marinated in crushed garlic, salt and pepper

1.5 L (2½ pt) water

12-15 cloves garlic, crushed

1 large onion, grated

2 bunches fresh coriander (cilantro)

Red chillies (hot peppers) to taste, chopped

500 g (1 lb) dried prawns (shrimp) soaked in water for 12 hours or use 4 oz (125 g) prawn paste

250 g (8 oz) crunchy groundnut (peanut) paste or butter

Farinhe de mandioca (coarse cassava powder)

500 mL (¾ pt) coconut milk mixed with 250 mL (8 fl oz) water

250 mL (8 fl oz) dênde (palm) oil

*This Bahian dish is another that I am sure had its origins in West Africa. It is very similar to Nkatsebe, the groundnut (peanut) or palmnut mixed stew that is popular in the Akan region of Ghana.*

*Bahia is situated on the north-eastern coast of Brazil and is the country's most African state since most of its inhabitants can trace their origins through the slave trade to West Africa, particularly Nigeria.*

In a frying pan, heat the olive oil and cook the chicken pieces. Add the water and cook the chicken until it is tender. Remove the bones and set aside the chicken meat. Leave the stock in the pan. Add garlic, onion, coriander (cilantro) and chillies (hot peppers). Bring to the boil.

Drain the soaked prawns (shrimp) and mince them. Mix the paste with the farinhe de mandioca (coarse cassava powder). Add the minced prawn (shrimp), the groundnut (peanut) paste and flour mix and the coconut milk and water to the stock.

Stir constantly for 2–3 minutes until the stock thickens. Add the chicken meat and the dênde (palm) oil. Gently simmer for a further 3–4 minutes, stirring regularly to avoid sticking or burning. Serve with steamed rice, with baked sweet potato, yams or by itself.

*Note:* You can substitute fish for chicken.

SERVES 6–8

# BLACK-EYED BEAN AND PRAWN (SHRIMP) STEW WITH DENDE OIL

500 g (1 lb) dried, black-eyed beans

Salt to taste

250 mL (8 fl oz) dênde (palm) oil

3 large onions, cut thinly into strips

315 g (10 oz) tomatoes, blanched, peeled and diced

2–3 fresh red chillies (hot peppers), diced (optional)

220 g (7 oz) dried prawns (shrimp)

*The ubiquitous black-eyed bean is as widely travelled as the people who eat it. Appearing here in a Brazilian dish, it is also a staple dietary item in many regions of Africa due to its importance as an inexpensive and long-lasting secondary protein. Wherever African food has travelled, black-eyed beans have been part of the luggage!*

Soak the black-eyed beans in plenty of water overnight. Rinse the beans well with fresh water then boil them in a large saucepan, with plenty of water and a dash of salt. Cook for 30–40 minutes or until the beans are soft but not mushy. Drain the beans and set them aside.

In a separate large cooking pot, heat the oil. Sauté the onions until just golden. Add the tomatoes and chillies (hot peppers), stirring well to prevent burning. Cook for about 3 minutes on medium heat, stirring all the time. Add the dried prawns (shrimp) and stir. Turn down the heat and cook for 3 more minutes. Stir in the cooked beans and simmer for 10–15 minutes before serving.

Serve with grilled or fried plantains or bananas, boiled brown or white rice, coarsely grated, dry-baked cassava or farinhe de mandioca (coarse cassava powder) (page 30).

SERVES 4

# CHIN-CHIN OF CHICKEN

1 whole 2 kg (5 lb) chicken

Salt to taste

6–8 cloves garlic, crushed

125 mL (4 fl oz) olive oil

15 mL (1 tablespoon) dênde (palm) oil

15 g (1 tablespoon) grated root ginger

2 onions, finely chopped

125 g (4 oz) dried prawns (shrimp), ground

*This is yet another recipe that shows its African beginnings. To this day a similar recipe that uses fish instead of chicken is cooked in Ghana, where it is served with cornmeal dumplings such as Banku (page 24) instead of rice.*

Cut the chicken into pieces. Season with salt and garlic and marinate for at least 2 hours, preferably longer.

In a frying pan, heat the olive oil and fry the chicken pieces until they turn golden. Strain off excess oil and add the dênde (palm) oil, ginger, onions and prawns (shrimp). Cook gently until the chicken is tender. It may be necessary to add some water to stop it burning. Add small amounts of hot water at a time because this dish needs to be reasonably dry. Serve with steamed rice.

SERVES 6–8

# FEIJOADA
### BLACK BEAN STEW

500 g (1 lb) dried black beans or black-eyed beans

500 g (1 lb) dried beef or South African biltong from a specialist butcher

500 g (1 lb) salted pork

500 g (1 lb) salted pork spare ribs (cured or smoked hock)

2 pigs' trotters

300 g (9½ oz) salted pig's ear

2 Portuguese beef sausages, grilled and sliced, or salami

150 g (5 oz) smoked bacon (in 1 piece not sliced)

1 smoked beef tongue, cooked and sliced

30 g (2 tablespoons) lard or butter

2 large onions, diced

3 cloves garlic, crushed

2 red capsicums (sweet or bell peppers), diced

4–5 large tomatoes, blanched, peeled and diced

1 bay leaf

Freshly ground black pepper to taste

Chilli (hot pepper) powder to taste

6–10 shallots (spring onions) and a bunch of parsley tied together

Traditionally served in hotels in Rio de Janeiro for Saturday lunch, this black bean stew is generally considered to be Brazil's national dish. Feijoada has the longest list of ingredients I've ever seen and seems to use every leftover in the kitchen, but the result of the great variety of foods used is to make it absolutely unique and mouthwatering!

Soak the black beans overnight in plenty of water. In a separate pot soak the dried beef or biltong, salted pork, salted spare ribs, pigs' trotters and salted pig's ear. Cook the beans in plenty of water. Drain the meats, cover with water again and parboil. Drain and set aside. When the beans have cooked for 20 minutes, add the parboiled meats, the grilled sausages, the smoked bacon and the tongue. Cook slowly, add more water if necessary and salt to taste.

In a large pot, melt the lard. Sauté the onions and garlic until the onions are or bell golden. Add the capsicums (sweet peppers), tomatoes, bay leaf, black pepper, chilli powder, and shallots (spring onions) and parsley tied together as a 'garni' (this will be removed later). Cook slowly then add 2 ladlefuls of beans, mash together well (avoiding the 'garni'), then transfer to the remaining cooked beans and meat.

Stir everything together and continue cooking until the sauce thickens and the meats are well cooked. Taste for seasoning and remove the shallot (spring onion) and parsley 'garni'. Serve the bean stew and the cooked meats separately, with boiled white rice and Spicy Sauce.

*SPICY SAUCE*

**2 onions, diced**

**3 red chillies (hot peppers), finely chopped**

**1 teaspoon vinegar**

**Juice of 2–3 lemons**

**Salt to taste**

**2 shallots (spring onions), chopped**

**125 mL (4 oz) olive oil**

**60 g (2oz) parsley, chopped**

To make the sauce, combine all the ingredients in a gravy boat. Just before serving, add a ladleful of strained liquid from the stew.

Serve Feijoada with sauce, boiled white rice, sliced ripe oranges (peeled and rindless) and finely shredded 'couvé'.

*Note:* Couvé is a green-leafed vegetable. The nearest substitute is Chinese broccoli. However, if you are unable to find that, use spinach (silver beet). Roll the leaves tightly and slice very thinly. Quickly stir-fry in a little bit of vegetable oil with crushed garlic, add salt to taste and serve.

SERVES 8

# A CULINARY DEPARTURE

The links to West Africa are still strong in Bahia: not only in religion and dress (many black women still dress as their African counterparts do), but also in food, although Bahian cuisine has been strongly influenced by the Portuguese.

Like the West Africans, the Bahians favour palm oil (called dénde oil in Brazil), beans and coarse cassava powder (called gari in West Africa but farinhe de mandioca in Brazil) in many of their recipes. Some dishes are almost identical, like the Bahian fish dish called 'moquecan', which is prepared in virtually the same way as West African fish recipes and is even served with a similar sauce made from chillies (hot peppers) and palm oil.

While the origins are obvious, the Bahian cuisine does show what can evolve over distance and time. For example, unlike African cooking in which chillies and herbs are added during the preparation, in Bahia these flavourings are added last; as well, the use of coconut milk, spices and even fruits — mixing the sweet with the savoury — shows a departure from traditional African cuisine.

# TRINIDAD AND TOBAGO

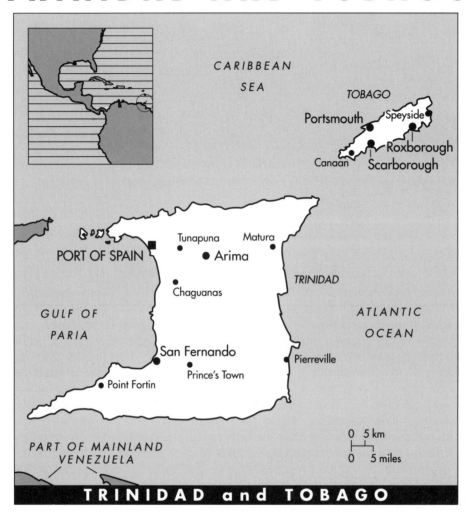

**TRINIDAD and TOBAGO**

**Official title**   Republic of Trinidad and Tobago

**Capital city**   Port of Spain

**Official language**   English, although French, Spanish, Hindi and Chinese are spoken

**Currency**   Trinidad and Tobago dollar (TT$) = 100 cents

**Cash crops for export**   Sugar, coffee, cocoa, coconuts and fresh fruits

**Food crops**   Sugar, beans, sweet potatoes and other vegetables, coconuts and fruit. Rice and meat are imported.

**Total land area**   Trinidad: 4828 sq km; Tobago: 300 sq km

# CALLALOO

SPINACH (SILVER BEET) SOUP

1 bunch of dasheen or spinach (silverbeet), finely chopped including stalks

1 pigs' tail or salted meat, cut in pieces (for seasoning only)

2 medium crabs or 250 g (½ lb) crab meat

250 mL (8 fl oz) coconut milk

1.5 L (2½ pt) water

1 onion, diced

2 cloves garlic

Salt and pepper to taste

250–300 g (8–10 oz) fresh baby okro (okra)

*This is the local Trinidadian name for a soup based on two varieties of spinach, locally known as 'dasheen'. The first is the 'elephant ear' — shaped leaves of the cocoyam (taro), common to West Africa, too, while the other is a local Trinidadian variety of spinach. Spinach (silver beet) can be substituted.*

*This soup is usually part of the tradition of Sunday feasting after going to church.*

Place all the ingredients except the crab meat and okros (okra) in a large soup pot and simmer on low heat until the pigs' tail or salted meat is tender. If you are using live crabs, add them with the other ingredients at the beginning. When the meat is tender, add the okro (okra) and crab meat if live crabs are not being used. Season and simmer until the okro (okra) seeds become darkish pink and the soup is thick. Serve hot with Foofoo, the Trinidadian equivalent to Fufu (page 13), just as it is in Trinidad, Tobago and West Africa!

SERVES 4

# BULJOL
SALTFISH SALAD

500 g (1 lb) salted fish

1 onion, diced

2 tomatoes, diced

5 g (1 teaspoon) fresh thyme

Chopped chives

Pepper to taste

60 mL (4 tablespoons) olive oil

30 mL (2 tablespoons) lime juice

*This fish salad is usually eaten with Bake (page 122), a bread-like biscuit. I have been told by my Trinidadian friend Annette Holton about a shop in San Fernando owned by old Mrs Tuckoor (affectionately known as Mummy Daph) for which workmen made a beeline every morning to buy their daily Bake and Buljol.*

Soak the saltfish in boiling water to remove excess salt, changing the water several times. When all the salt has been removed, shred the fish and remove any excess water and the bones. Place the shredded fish in a bowl and mix with the onion, tomatoes, thyme, chives and pepper to taste. Lastly, add olive oil and lime juice. This gives it a nice, moist, finishing touch.

*Note:* As a variation, add chopped mushrooms and avocados to the Buljol before serving.

SERVES 4–6

## THE LAND OF THE HUMMINGBIRD

It was only on Christopher Columbus's third voyage to the Caribbean region that he discovered Trinidad in 1498. This small island and its even smaller satellite, Tobago, lie between the southern tail of the Windward group of islands and just a few kilometres from the coast of Venezuala, separated from it by two sea channels: Dragon's Mouth and Serpent's Mouth.

Trinidad was originally called 'Iere' or 'the land of the hummingbird' by its original Amerindia inhabitants, the Arawaks and the Caribs.

# PELAU
PIGEON PEAS AND RICE

**60 mL (4 tablespoons) vegetable oil**

**15 g (1 tablespoon) brown sugar**

**500 g (1 lb) meat or chicken, cut in chunks**

**250 g (½ lb) long-grain rice**

**125 g (4 oz) peas or beans, of your choice**

**125 mL (4 fl oz) coconut milk**

**Salt and pepper to taste**

*SEASONING*

**Queen of herbs, garlic, parsley, onions, salt and chives.**

*Pelau is a popular dish throughout the Caribbean. Pigeon peas (also known in Jamaica as gungo peas) are actually beans, not peas, and are of African origin. You can buy pigeon peas fresh or dried.*

In a large cooking pot, or saucepan, heat the oil. Add the brown sugar and stir until it has almost caramelised. Add the meat or chicken with a little water and simmer until the meat is half cooked. Stir in the long-grain rice, peas or beans and coconut milk.

Stir and season to taste. Simmer on low heat for 20–25 minutes or until everything is cooked and moist but not soggy. Serve hot with stews and roasts.

SERVES 4

# CARNIVAL

A tradition brought to Trinidad by the French sugarcane planters who were escaping slave uprisings on the French island colonies of Martinique and Haiti in the mid-eighteenth century, Carnival has a long history in Trinidad.

The original celebrations which lasted from Christmas to Ash Wednesday originally excluded the black slaves. While the French plantation owners would paint their faces black and dress up as field slaves (negré jardin) and dance to African drum rhythms, slaves only participated to provide entertainment for their owners.

The abolition of the slave trade in 1834 freed the slaves to celebrate their own carnivals. Drawing on their ancestral West African traditions so that well known figures and rituals such as Shango, Mama Deleau (Mami Water in Ghana), and the Kalinda stick dance and Bamboula became integral, and by adding to them acquired European rituals and dances, Carnival became the spectacular annual shows they are today.

# COOCOO
STEAMED CORNMEAL

Salt to taste

1¾ L (3 pt) water

10–16 young fresh okro (okra) topped and tailed

60 g (4 tablespoons) butter

250 g (½ lb) cornmeal

Tomatoes, green capsicums (sweet or bell peppers), parsley, etc, to garnish

*There are innumerable ways of preparing this recipe for steamed cornmeal — it all depends which island you take the recipe from; this one is from Tobago. One thing that all the recipes for steamed cornmeal have in common is that they are derived from the African version, variously known as Banku, Ugali, Sadza and Mealie-meal, and Nsima, among others.*

Add the salt to the water and bring to the boil in a large pot. Slice the okro (okra) into thick rings and drop them into the boiling water. Add half the butter and gently pour in the cornmeal. Stir in well to avoid lumps. Lower the heat and continue stirring for 5–10 minutes until the cornmeal has absorbed most of the water and is cooked.

Grease a serving dish with the remaining butter. Tip the Coocoo into the dish and swirl it about to form a ball. Garnish with the tomatoes, capsicums (sweet or bell peppers), parsley and other salad vegetables of your choice. Serve with fried, steamed or baked fish or by itself. In Trinidad, Coocoo is often made with 125 g (4 oz) cooked, whole corn (maize) kernels added.

SERVES 4

# DUMPLINGS

125 g (4 oz) flour, (plain and cornmeal mixed in equal quantities)

Salt to taste

10 g (2 teaspoons) baking powder

5 g (1 teaspoon) herb or spice of your choice (optional)

15 g (1 tablespoon) butter

Water

*These are popular in the West Indies where the recipes vary depending upon whether the dumplings are being made to accompany a soup or a stew. This particular version is meant to go with a soup such as Callaloo (page 117).*

In a bowl mix the flours with the salt, baking powder and the herbs or spices you are using. Rub in the butter thoroughly. Gradually add very small amounts of water until the flour becomes a soft dough.

Break off small pieces of dough and roll into finger-size shapes. Drop these shapes into soup to cook.

*Note:* Some people prefer to make their dumplings plain, by excluding the butter and baking powder. Alternatively, you can make more elaborate dumplings by including numerous herbs and spices like mixed spice or herbs, nutmeg, crushed red chillies (hot peppers), fresh, finely chopped basil, and so forth.

SERVES 4

---

## 'T&T'

Trinidad was initially colonised by the Spanish, who had control for almost 300 years, although during this time French and Dutch settlements periodically sprang up. Power over the island was wrested from the Spanish by the British in 1797 during the Napoleonic wars. In contrast to the relative stability of rule in Trinidad, neighbouring Tobago changed hands between the Spanish, British, French and Dutch many times in just over 200 years. Finally in 1888 Tobago became a ward of Trinidad.

All the colonisers were no doubt eager to exploit the fertile terrain and excellent climate in order to grow sugar cane and cocoa. African slave labour was used until the trade was abolished in 1834, when indentured labour from India and Asia was brought in to work on the estates, all adding to the extraordinarily diverse racial and cultural mix that still makes up 'T & T's' population today.

# BAKE

**250 g (½ lb) plain flour**

**Salt to taste**

**10 g (2 teaspoons) baking powder**

**60 g (4 tablespoons) butter**

**Coconut milk**

**Vegetable oil for frying**

*There are three traditional ways of cooking this Trinidad and Tobago-style of bread-like biscuit: it can be fried, baked or cooked, generally on a coalpot or on a griddle. Mummy Daph (see recipe introduction on page 118) used to make Bakes to go with Buljol on the top of a coalpot. A coalpot is like a small coal-fired barbecue, but western cooks can use oil in a frypan.*

Sift flour, salt and baking powder together in a bowl. Rub in the butter until the flour is crumbly. Add small amounts of coconut milk and knead together to form a dough.

Roll out the dough on a floured board to make a large flat round. Prick all over with a fork to facilitate quick baking. Place on a hot griddle or tarwa or cook in hot oil in frypan until both sides are brown. Serve hot with Buljol or other fish, meat or vegetables of your choice.

SERVES 2

## CALYPSO

A uniquely Trinidadian form of music, calypso evolved from the drum rhythms brought from Africa during the slave trade and the melodic influence of French and Spanish colonisers. The lyric element of calypso first derived from the folk chant of the West African people, but soon developed into long and taunting songs that satirised their colonial masters, passed on gossip and unified the sense of identity of the people. These days calypso songs still have a strong satirical edge and are frequently composed spontaneously and sung in dialect.

Steel bands are an integral part of calypso and originated in Trinidad, too. Also evolving from the African drum heritage, metal drums were used when, under British rule, African drums were banned. The metal containers are cut into various sizes to produce different pitches and then hammered into sections to allow separate notes to be sounded. So sophisticated are steel drums today, that practically any style of music can be played upon them.

# MARTINIQUE AND GUADELOUPE

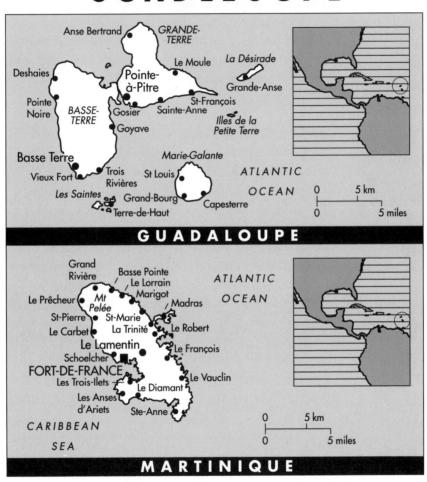

**Official title**  Martinique and Guadeloupe

**Capital city**  Fort de France (Martinique) and Basse Terre (Guadeloupe)

**Official language**  French, although English and Creole are spoken

**Currency**  French franc (FF) = 100 centimes

**Cash crops for export**  Sugar, bananas and pineapples

**Food crops**  Sugar, rice, fresh fruits, vegetables, livestock and fish

**Total land area**  Martinique: 1100 sq km; Guadeloupe: 1780 sq km

# ESCARGOTS

**Salt to taste**

**1.5 L (2½ pt) water**

**8-12 snails or 500 g (1 lb) canned escargots**

**125 g (4 oz) butter**

**2 onions, diced**

**3 cloves garlic, diced**

**2-4 red chillies (hot peppers), diced, or paprika (optional)**

**250g (½ lb) mushrooms, cleaned and quartered**

**250g (½ lb) spinach (silverbeet), washed and very finely sliced**

**10 g (2 teaspoons) freshly ground black pepper**

**250 mL (8 fl oz) thick (double) cream**

*Snails are very popular in West Africa where they grow to phenomenal sizes in the rainforests. The biggest snails come from the Ivory Coast. They are used fresh in soups and vegetable stews or are dried and salted to preserve them for eating later in the season when fresh snails are scarcer. This recipe from Martinique and Guadeloupe is a very French way of preparing snails.*

Add the salt to the water and bring to the boil in a large pot. Drop in the snails and cook for 20–30 minutes until they are done. Drain the snails and soak in cold water for 10 minutes to cool. Remove their shells and pull off the entrails and all the slimy attachments to the main black body. Cut the cleaned snails into halves down the full length of the body. They are now ready to be incorporated into the recipe. If you decide to use canned escargots, open the can and drain them.

In a large cooking pot, melt the butter and sauté the onions, garlic, chillies (hot peppers) and mushrooms for 10–15 minutes. Add the snails and spinach (silver beet) and cook for another 10–15 minutes, stirring continuously. Add salt to taste and stir in the freshly ground black pepper and cream. Cook for a further 5–10 minutes. Serve hot with plain boiled long-grain rice and fresh green vegetables of your choice.

SERVES 4

# MATÉTÉ DES CRABES
CRABS IN RICE

155 mL (5 fl oz) olive oil

1 kg (2 lb) crab meat

2 large onions, diced

4 cloves garlic, diced

2–3 red chillies (hot peppers), diced

Herbs e.g. oregano, thyme or chives (optional)

Salt to taste

400 g (13 oz) long-grain rice

2–3 bay leaves

1 L (1¾ pt) vegetable stock or water mixed with 2 vegetable stock cubes

Garnish of your choice

Juice of 1 lemon

*This is another West Indian dish in which you can easily recognise the African ancestry. It is like the Seafood or Crab Jollof Rice to be found in Sierra Leone or Liberia, or a gari (coarse cassava powder) and crab dish that is favoured in Ghana, Togo, Benin or Nigeria.*

*Matété de Crabes is from Guadeloupe and is cooked very quickly with spices in the French way.*

In a heavy-based saucepan, heat the oil and toss in the crab meat, onions, garlic, chillies (hot peppers), herbs and salt. Cook over medium heat, stirring continuously for 5–10 minutes, being careful not to let the crab meat break up. Add the rice, bay leaves and vegetable stock. Adjust seasoning to taste. Cover and cook on very low heat for 20–30 minutes or until the rice is cooked and has absorbed all the water. You may need to add more water depending on the type of rice used. Remove bay leaves and serve.

Serve hot arranged on lettuce leaves and garnished with sliced hard-boiled eggs or a mixture of sliced cucumbers and tomatoes topped with chopped chives and lemon juice.

SERVES 4

## CREOLE

A unique combination of French, Spanish and African heritages have evolved into the culture of Creole. A term originally used in Latin America, Creole distinguished the descendants of the European colonisers from the Amerindians, Africans and later immigrants. Over time these groups have mixed and today Creole has formed a unique part of the culture, particularly in Martinique, Guadeloupe and Louisiana. The resultant cuisine is a celebrated blend of African vegetable and fish ingredients; the clever use of spices and herbs, so much a style of Spain; and the refined sauces of France. While the strong African signature remains, the heavy emphasis on onions, ginger and large quantities of chillies, which are integral to African cooking, have been replaced by the roux and piquant sauces of French and Spanish Creoles.

# SAUTÉ DE POULET AU COCO
## SAUTÉED CHICKEN IN COCONUT MILK

4-6 quarters of chicken (breasts, wings or thighs) or 6-8 drumsticks

30 g (2 tablespoons) plain flour mixed with 15 g (1 tablespoon) salt

250 mL (8 fl oz) vegetable oil

500 mL (¾ pt) coconut milk

1 onion, diced

2 red cloves garlic, diced

250 g (½ lb) whole, button or small mushrooms

2 red chillies (hot peppers), diced (optional)

Garlic or celery salt to taste (optional)

*Chicken and coconut dishes lend themselves to individual touches. This is the basic recipe from Martinique and Guadeloupe, so feel free to experiment: add some wine or some lime juice — who knows, you may discover an inspired version!*

Clean the chicken and dry with paper towel. Season with the flour and salt mix. Heat the oil in a large cooking pot and fry the chicken until golden. Remove from the heat and pour the excess oil into a separate pan; set aside.

Return the chicken pieces to the stove in the same pot without rinsing it – the browned base retains chicken juices and adds flavour. Add the coconut milk and simmer on very low heat. Using the leftover oil sauté the onion, garlic, mushrooms and chillies (hot peppers) until the onions soften and brown. Add to the simmering chicken in the coconut milk. Season to taste with celery or garlic salt. Continue to simmer gently until the chicken is tender and the sauce has thickened. Serve hot with rice and sliced fresh tomatoes.

SERVES 4

# PORC AVEC AUBERGINES
PORK WITH EGGPLANT (AUBERGINE)

125 mL (4 fl oz) groundnut (peanut) oil

4–6 lean pork fillets

60 g (4 tablespoons) plain flour mixed with salt to taste

40 mL (²/₃ pt) water

Spices of your choice

5 g (1 teaspoon) paprika

4 medium eggplants (aubergines) or 8–10 garden eggs (a small, white tropical version of eggplant), peeled and diced

2 fresh apples, diced (optional)

*Pork and eggplant (aubergine) might seem strange bedfellows, but in West Africa we regularly combine the two in our cooking. Adding apples creates an even more unusual flavour. It's when you blend ingredients together in an exotic way that you know you are 'eating with many tongues'!*

Heat the oil in a heavy-based pan. Coat the pork with the combined flour and salt, and sauté in the oil until golden. Add the water, spices, and paprika and simmer on low heat until the meat is tender. Stir in the eggplant (aubergine) and apples and cook for about 20 minutes or until everything is cooked and sauce is thickened. Serve hot with rice, mashed yams or potatoes.

SERVES 4

## OF FLOWERS AND BEAUTIFUL WATERS

Some of the original Amerindian inhabitants of the Caribbean, the Caribs, called Martinique the 'island of flowers'. Its sister island, Guadeloupe, lying 320 km (200 miles) north, was called 'Karukera' or 'the island of beautiful waters' by its original Arawak Indians. Guadeloupe's name was changed with Christopher Columbus charted it in 1493 and called it Santa Maria de Guadeloupe de Estramaduros.

Guadeloupe is actually comprised of two small islands, Grande Terre to the east and Bass Terre to the west, separated by a sea channel called the Riviére Salée.

Martinique and Guadeloupe form the western most boundary of French territory because both are departments of France.

# RATATOUILLE CRÉOLE

**185 mL (6 fl oz) olive oil**

**2 onions, sliced into thin rings**

**2 each red and green capsicums (sweet or bell peppers), seeded and sliced into thick strips**

**500 g (1 lb) zucchini (courgettes), chopped**

**2 large cucumbers, peeled and thickly sliced**

**2 medium eggplants (aubergines), peeled and chopped**

**500 g (1 lb) tomatoes, blanched, peeled and thickly sliced**

**Salt and black pepper to taste**

**5 g (1 teaspoon) mixed herbs**

**Sugar to taste (optional)**

*This dish reminds me of Zimbabwean cucumber and pumpkin dishes. Although cucumber is not generally eaten in other African countries it is sometimes used in vegetable-combination stews depending upon local availability. Cucumber is common to Martinique and Guadeloupe, however, and lends itself beautifully to the ratatouille.*

Pour the olive oil into a very large ovenproof dish, add the onions, cover and cook for 10 minutes in an oven preheated to 200°C (400°F). Remove from the oven and arrange other vegetables attractively in layers on top of the onion. Season to taste.

Cover and cook in the oven for 10 minutes then uncover and add the herbs and sugar. Continue cooking for 20–30 minutes until all the ingredients are cooked and any juices have reduced. This dish must be moist not dry. Serve hot either by itself or as an accompaniment to baked or roast fish or meat dishes.

SERVES 4–6

**From Cuba** Frijoles Negros con Pescado (Black-eyed Beans with Fish) (page 142)

# POIS ROUGES MACONNE
RICE AND PEAS GUADELOUPE STYLE

60 mL (4 tablespoons) groundnut (peanut) oil

1 large onion,

2 cloves garlic, diced

1–2 red chillies (hot peppers), diced

4 rashers bacon, (chopped)

375 g (¾ lb) red kidney beans, soaked in water for 1 hour then well rinsed

Salt and pepper to taste

1 L (1¾ pt) water

250 g (½ lb) long-grain rice

30 g (2 tablespoons) farine de manioc (coarse cassava powder)

*Rice and Peas is almost as synonymous with the West Indies as cricket and, like cricket, each island has its own special way of cooking them. This particular recipe from Guadelope is different from any other rice-and-pea combinations I have come across. Actually the combination is of rice and beans, but for some unknown reason it is called rice and peas all over the Caribbeen. Apart from the intrigue with the name, I discovered it originated from the gari (coarse cassava powder) and bean dishes of Africa but had evolved with tasty additions of bacon, garlic and rice. I have been hooked ever since.*

In a pan heat the oil and gently saut  the onion, garlic, red chillies (hot peppers) and bacon until the bacon is cooked but not browned. Add rinsed beans, salt and water. Bring to the boil and simmer for 45 minutes to 1 hour until the beans are semi-cooked. Add the rice, season to taste and stir well to mix. Cover and simmer on very low heat until both the rice and the beans are cooked and soft. You may need to add more water at this stage to help the rice cook if there is not enough, but be careful not to make it too soggy.

Stir in the farine de manioc (coarse cassava powder) to absorb any remaining fluid and to thicken the sauce. Leave on very low heat for a further 5 minutes before serving. Serve as hot as you wish.

SERVES 4

# JEUNNE BANANES AUX SAUCE
BABY PLANTAINS IN SAUCE

**4–8 unripe baby plantains**

**Salt and pepper to taste**

**125 g (4 oz) butter**

**60–75 g (3–4 tablespoons) plain flour**

**375 mL (13 fl oz) milk**

**125 g (4 oz) Parmesan or other strong, grated cheese**

**5 g (1 teaspoon) ground nutmeg**

*Just as they are in Africa, plantains are a favourite of the French Caribbean Islands, although more often than not they are eaten as a sweet and not used as a savoury. Contrarily that is why I chose this savoury plantain recipe from Martinique.*

Oil your hands slightly to prevent the plantain juice from staining them. Score the plantains lengthwise with a sharp knife. Peel off the green skins and extract the baby plantains whole.

Rinse and place the plantains in a saucepan. Cover with cold water, sprinkle with salt and bring to the boil. Cook for 15–20 minutes or until the plantains soften. Remove from the heat and drain off the water. Arrange the cooked plantains in a deep, buttered ovenproof dish, set aside and keep warm.

In a deep frypan, melt the butter over low heat. Stir in the plain flour and mix well to form a roux. Pour in the milk, stirring continuously until it thickens into a smooth, white sauce. Season to taste with salt and pepper. Pour evenly to cover the plantains, top with grated cheese and sprinkle nutmeg over the top. Cook, uncovered, for 10–15 minutes in an oven preheated to 200°C (400°F). Serve as hot as you wish.

SERVES 4

# JAMAICA

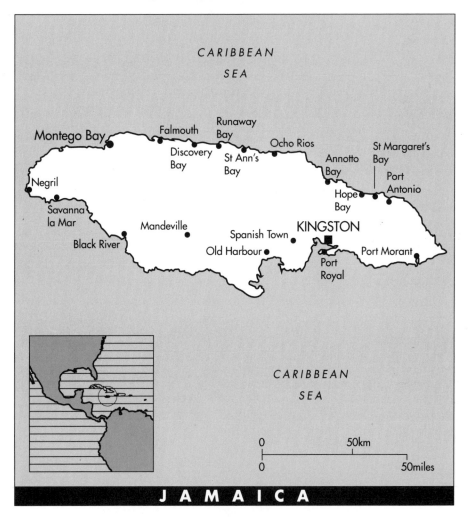

CARIBBEAN SEA

Montego Bay
Falmouth
Runaway Bay
Ocho Rios
St Margaret's Bay
Discovery Bay
St Ann's Bay
Annotto Bay
Port Antonio
Negril
Hope Bay
Savanna la Mar
Mandeville
KINGSTON
Black River
Spanish Town
Old Harbour
Port Morant
Port Royal

CARIBBEAN SEA

0        50km
0        50miles

## JAMAICA

**Official title**   Jamaica

**Capital city**   Kingston

**Official language**   English, although Creole and Patois are widely spoken

**Currency**   Jamaican dollar (J$) = 100 cents

**Cash crops for export**   Sugar, cocoa, coffee, citrus fruits, bananas, pimentoes and ginger

**Food crops**   Rice, yams, bananas, other fruits, vegetables, livestock and fish

**Total land area**   Approximately 11, 000  sq km

# ACKEE AND SALTFISH

**500 g (1 lb) salted fish**

**45 mL (3 tablespoons) vegetable oil**

**2 onions, diced**

**125 g (4 oz) piece of smoked hock or bacon, diced**

**2 red or green capsicums (sweet or bell peppers), diced**

**3 tomatoes, diced**

**Fresh basil, finely chopped or a pinch of dried oregano**

**Salt and pepper to taste**

**470 g (15 oz) canned ackee, drained**

**Garnish, e.g. tomatoes, onion, parsley, fresh coriander**

*This well-known Jamaican dish reminds me of a Ghanaian favourite called Koobi Ne Kosua Froye, which my mother used to make for me. So popular is Ackee and Saltfish in Jamaica that it has reached the status of national dish and songs have been written about ackee.*

*Ackee is the edible yellow fruit found in the seed pods of a tropical West African tree (Blighia sapida) that now grows in Jamaica. It is difficult to obtain fresh ackee outside Africa and Jamaica, but the tinned fruit can be found. Fresh ackee should not be eaten unless it comes from a fully opened seed pod and has been cooked.*

Soak the salted fish overnight to remove excess salt then rinse in cold water. Bone, skin and flake it into small pieces.

In a frying pan, heat the oil and sauté the onions for about 3 minutes. Add the smoked hock or bacon, capsicums (sweet or bell peppers), tomatoes, basil or oregano and seasoning.

Gently cook for about 3–5 minutes stirring regularly. Add the flaked fish and cook for a further 5–10 minutes. Stir in the drained ackee, mix well and cook on low heat for another 10 minutes. Stir gently but regularly to prevent burning. Serve hot with rice and the garnish of your choice.

SERVES 4

# CHICKEN WITH RUM AND COCONUT

12 chicken wings or small drumsticks

60 g (4 tablespoons) butter

90 mL (3 fl oz) vegetable oil

60-90 mL (2-3 fl oz) Jamaican rum

2-3 chicken stock cubes, crushed

Garlic powder (amount optional)

Freshly ground black pepper to taste

400 mL (⅔ pt) coconut cream

300 mL (½ pt) cream

220 g (7 oz) small, mushrooms, washed

*It would be criminal to write about my favourite Jamaican recipes and not include this popular one that uses the rum that Jamaica produces to perfection. Chicken with Rum and Coconut is very rich and designed to impress.*

Clean the chicken wings, cut off and discard the little jointed finger-like tips. Cut each wing in half to produce a flat part and a fleshy mini drumstick.

In a heavy-based saucepan, heat the butter and oil. Sauté the chicken wings until golden and cooked . You may have to fry in small batches. When all the chicken wings are cooked, return them to the pan on the stove and lower the heat. This next part is tricky so be careful.

Quickly pour the rum over the chicken wings and light a match to set the rum alight. Carefully tilt the pan to ensure all the chicken wings are flambéed.

When the flames die down, add the chicken stock cubes, garlic powder, lots of freshly ground black pepper, the coconut cream and the cream. Stir well to mix and simmer gently. Add the mushrooms and simmer on low to medium heat until the sauce thickens.

Serve hot with boiled rice tossed through with mixed herbs, and fresh steamed vegetables of your choice.

SERVES 4

# THE LANGUAGE CONNECTION

Jamaica's earliest settlers were the Arawak Indians and the name of the island today derives from the Arawak word 'Xaymaca' which means 'island of the springs'. It is commonplace to describe the Amerindians of the Caribbean as the 'peaceful' Arawaks and the 'warlike' Caribs, but whatever their dispositions, neither group lasted long after European colonisation began.

What has remained as a constant reminder of these people is fragments of their languages, which are still in use today. Besides the names of the islands Jamaica, Cuba and Martinique, words such as tobacco, hammock, canoe, hurricane, iguana, maize and potato have endured.

Also enduring in the language of many Caribbean islands are examples of the languages carried by slaves from several different African countries. Many have been modified over time, to be sure, but there are innumerable examples of words from different African languages such as Yoruba and Ashanti that still exist in the melting pot of Jamaica.

Examples include Fufu, the name of a dumpling popular in both West African and West Indian countries (it is sometimes spelled 'foofoo'); abé, the edible seed of the palmnut; ackee, the favourite breakfast fruit of Jamaica, which originally came from West Africa; abeng, a style of wind instrument made from a bull's horn; the kumina, a form of an Ashanti ancestral possession cult, which in Ghana is called 'Akom-ina'; and patu, the name for an owl.

Personal names also still form a link between the language of the African heritage and the Jamaicans of today. Recorded in history are the names of Maroon generals and chiefs such as Cudjoe, Quao, Nana Acheampong and Taky, which are still names in current use in Ghana. Another example is the name Quashie, which in Africa is Kwesi (pronounced 'Quarshie'); the spelling and pronunciation might have evolved over time and distance, but the African heritage remains.

# JERK PORK

1.5 kg (3 lb) pork fillets, thickly sliced

MARINADE

4 red chillies (hot peppers), diced

2 onions, diced

1 large piece root ginger, peeled and grated

60 g (4 tablespoons) hot chilli paste (e.g. Sambal Oelek)

125 mL (4 fl oz) vegetable oil

5 g (1 teaspoon) allspice

60 mL (4 tablespoons) soya sauce

5 g (1 teaspoon) garlic salt

3 bay leaves

*There is no specific English meaning for the word 'jerk' in this Jamaican specialty. 'Jerking' is said to be a secret Arawak Indian method of cooking pig.*

*However, Jerk Pork is, tougue-in-cheek, pork with a 'kick': grilled pork with seasoning that makes it sit up and be noticed like the Ghanaian 'pedestrian' pork called Domedo. I believe that the present Jamaican Jerk Pork has evolved from original Arawak Indian and African versions. This recipe is a modified combination of Jerk Pork and Domedo.*

*Jerk Pork is so delicious that the anticipation of eating it is enough to make me click my fingers and shake my head with excitement. There doesn't seem to be a 'secret' recipe for Jerk Pork: cooks keep referring me to a ready-made 'jerk seasoning'.*

In a blender or food processor, blend the chillies (hot peppers), onions and ginger. If chilli paste is used then blend only the onions and ginger. Add all the other marinade ingredients and mix well. Rub over the pork, cover and marinate overnight.

Remove the pork from the marinade and barbecue over hot coals, or roast in an oven preheated to 180°C (350°F) until the pork is well cooked. Pour the marinade into a small saucepan, add 125 mL (4 fl oz) water and simmer gently on low heat for 10–15 minutes, stirring to prevent burning. When the pork is cooked, serve the sauce separately. This dish can be served with drinks or as a meal with salad and sweet potatoes, rice or breadfruit.

*Note:* As a variation, sprinkle small portions of cinnamon sticks, chicory, dried basil or some other herb on the barbecue coals so the pork absorbs these flavours.

SERVES 4–6

# STUFFED PAWPAW (PAPAYA)

60 mL (4 tablespoons) vegetable oil

2 onions, diced

3 cloves garlic, diced

2 red chillies (hot peppers) (optional)

500 g (1 lb) topside or lean minced beef

60 mL (4 tablespoons) water

10 g (2 teaspoons) tomato paste

2 tomatoes, blanched, peeled and diced

Salt and freshly ground black pepper to taste

500 g (1 lb) unripe pawpaw (papaya), peeled, seeded and halved

185 g (6 oz) Parmesan cheese, grated

4 tomatoes, washed and left whole

Finely chopped chives

Black pepper, finely ground

*Although in western countries pawpaw (papaya) is treated as a fruit, its versatility is exploited more in Africa and the West Indies. Like Africans, Jamaicans use the unripe, green, 'baby' pawpaws (papayas) as a substitute in the absence of eggplants (aubergines) and other vegetables.*

*In its soft, ripe, orange form, it is used the world over as a fruit or in puddings of various kinds.*

*Pawpaw (papaya) is another of the extremely beneficial fruits and vegetables that have both medicinal and culinary properties.*

Heat the oil in a saucepan and sauté the onions, garlic and chillies (hot peppers) for 5–7 minutes until onions are golden. Stir in the mince and cook for a further 10 minutes. Mix the water and tomato paste together and add with the diced tomatoes to the pan. Season with salt and pepper to taste. Cook on low heat for 10–15 minutes to thicken the mixture slightly. Remove from the heat and set aside.

Cover the pawpaw (papaya) halves in boiling water and steep for 10–15 minutes. Remove the pawpaw (papaya), drain and dry with paper towels. Lightly grease a baking dish and arrange pawpaw (papaya) halves side by side in it. Fill the halves with mince mixture and top with Parmesan.

Arrange the whole tomatoes around the pawpaw (papaya) halves and bake for for 30–45 minutes in an oven preheated to 200°C (400°F), until the pawpaw (papaya) is cooked. Serve hot, topped with chives and black pepper.

SERVES 4

# SWEET POTATO PONE

**1 kg (2 lb) sweet potatoes or yams, grated**

**250 g (8 oz) pumpkin, grated**

**15 g (3 teaspoons) grated root ginger**

**60 g (2 oz) butter, melted**

**125 g (4 oz) desiccated or freshly grated coconut**

**250 mL (8 fl oz) water**

**250 g (8 oz) cane or caster sugar**

**Vanilla essence to taste**

**Grated nutmeg to taste**

**60 g (2 oz) each sultanas and raisins (optional)**

*Pone can be made from cornmeal, sweet potatoes, yams or gari (coarse cassava powder), but my favourite recipe uses sweet potato. It can be eaten hot or cold, but I love it cold because the flavour of the ginger seems to become stronger.*

*Pone can be served as a dessert with cream, as an accompaniment to roast pork or poultry, or eaten hot or cold as a snack on its own.*

In a large mixing bowl, combine all ingredients and mix well. Grease 2 flan or pie dishes and pour in the mixture. Smooth the tops. Bake in an oven preheated to 180°C (350°F) for 1 hour. Serve hot or cold.

SERVES 4–6

# CORNMEAL PUDDING

1 small coconut or 250 mL (8 fl oz) coconut cream mixed with 650 mL (1pt) water

500 g (1 lb) yellow cornmeal or polenta

125–250 g (4–8 oz) sugar (depending on personal taste)

60 g (4 tablespoons) butter

Salt and spices to taste e.g. grated nutmeg, vanilla, cinnamon or allspice

*Cornmeal, like black-eyed beens, is a traditional part of soul food, whether it is found in the West Indies, Latin America, African-America, or Africa itself. With the addition of coconut and sugar (from sugarcane), the humble original cornmeal has taken on a sweet Jamaican identity that has become a delicious tradition in virtually every Jamaican home.*

Grate the coconut and squeeze out 900 mL (1½ pt) coconut milk or combine 250 mL (8 fl oz) tin of coconut cream with 650 mL (1 pt) of water. Blend with the remaining ingredients and pour the mixture into a buttered baking dish. Bake until cooked an oven preheated to 180–200°C (350–400°F). Remove from the oven, cool a little and serve.

SERVES 4

# AVOCADO ICE-CREAM

3 eggs

90 g (3 oz) caster sugar

475 mL (15 fl oz) milk

5 mL (1 teaspoon) vanilla essence

2 avocados, mashed with 1 teaspoon lemon juice and 60 g (4 tablespoons) caster sugar

*I know most people think of avocados as something to go in salads or soups or as a part of the main meal, but this recipe is proof that it can be made into an unusual and delicious pudding: ice-cream, in fact.*

To make the basic egg custard, lightly beat the eggs and sugar together. Bring the milk to nearly boiling point (it must not boil). Add the vanilla essence to the milk and quickly stir into the eggs and sugar mixture. Cook the custard in the top half of a double boiler over hot water. Stir continuously until the mixture thickens and coats the back of a spoon. Remove from the heat and cool.

When cool, combine the avocado mix with the custard. Stir well then chill in the freezer for 3–4 hours. Remove, beat well again to make it smoother and chill for a second time. Serve with the garnish of your choice.

SERVES 4

# CUBA

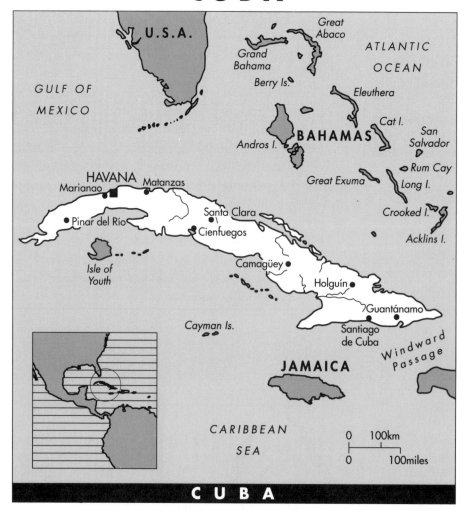

CUBA

**Official title**  Republic of Cuba

**Capital city**  Havana (Habana)

**Official language**  Spanish, although English is used in business

**Currency**  Cuban peso = 100 centavos

**Cash crops for export**  Sugar, cotton, tobacco and fish

**Food crops**  Rice, maize, cotton, cassava, sweet potatoes, potatoes, other vegetables, fruit, livestock and fish

**Total land area**  Approximately 114,500 sq km

# ARROZ CON PESCADO AL RON

RICE AND FISH IN RUM

## FISH STOCK

**Fish heads, tails etc**

**1.25 L (4 pt) water**

**1 bay leaf**

**1 small capsicum (sweet or bell pepper)**

**1 large onion**

**1 tomato**

**Salt to taste**
**½ teaspoon dried oregano or ground cumin**

**Salt to taste**

**5 g (1 teaspoon) freshly ground black pepper**

**15 g (1 tablespoon) ground cinnamon**

**90 mL (3 fl oz) lemon juice or vinegar**

**500 g (1 lb) favourite firm fish, boned and cut into big chunks**

**500 g (1 lb) rice**

**1 L (1 ¾ pt) fish stock (see recipe above)**

**125 mL (4 fl oz) vegetable oil**

**1 onion, diced**

**3 cloves garlic, diced**

**30 mL (2 tablespoons) mushroom soya sauce or Worcestershire sauce**

**125 mL (4 fl oz) rum**

**5 g (1 teaspoon) saffron or turmeric**

*I had to have this versatile and delicious recipe translated for me as it was in Spanish, given to me by Mrs Emilia Marchante of Cuba. It is versatile because you can vary the taste to suit yourself by adding different spices to it. I love it because it contains rice and rum!*

To make the fish stock, in a large pot simmer the ingredients for about 1 hour on medium to low heat. Remove from the heat, strain stock through a fine sieve and discard the solids.

To make the fish and rice in rum, combine the oregano or cumin, salt, pepper, cinnamon and lemon juice or vinegar. Marinate the fish in this mixture, covered, for 2–4 hours. Soak the rice in 500 mL (¾ pt) fish stock.

Heat the oil in a large cooking pot and sauté the onion and garlic for 3-5 minutes until they start to brown. Quickly add the mushroom soya or Worcestershire sauce and the fish with its marinade. Cook for 2–3 minutes. Add the rum, the remaining fish stock and the saffron or tumeric. Adjust the seasoning to taste. Lastly, add the steeped rice.

Stir well together, taking care not to break up the fish too much. Cook on very low heat for about 45 minutes or until the rice is cooked. You may need to add more water during the cooking process depending on whether you use white or brown rice. Serve hot with fresh vegetables of your choice.

SERVES 4

# FRIJOLES NEGROS CON PESCADO

BLACK-EYED BEANS WITH FISH

**500 g (1 lb) dried, black-eyed beans**

**Salt to taste**

**125 mL (4 fl oz) vegetable oil**

**4 large onions, diced**

**315 g (10 oz) tomatoes, blanched, peeled and diced**

**10 g (2 teaspoons) turmeric**

**2–3 red chillies (hot peppers), diced (optional)**

**250 g (½ lb) smoked or fried fish, boned, skinned and cut in small chunks**

**125 g (4 oz) dried prawns (shrimp)**

*The ever-popular and useful black-eyed bean pops up in recipes in Cuba, too. This time the beans are combined with smoked or fried fish — with a Spanish touch.*

Soak the black-eyed beans overnight in plenty of water. Rinse the beans with fresh water several times then boil them in a large saucepan, with plenty of salted water. Cook for 30–40 minutes or until the beans are soft but not mushy. Drain and set them aside.

In a separate large cooking pot, heat the oil. Fry the onions until golden, add the tomatoes, turmeric and chillies (hot peppers) and stir well to prevent burning. Cook for about 3 minutes on medium heat, stirring all the time. Add the fish and prawns (shrimp) and stir. Lower the heat and cook for 3 more minutes. Stir in the cooked beans and simmer for 10–15 minutes. Serve with grilled or fried plantains and boiled 'arroz blanco' white rice.

SERVES 4–6

# SALSA ROJA PARA FRIJOLE NEGROS
### RED SAUCE FOR BLACK-EYED BEANS

250 mL (8 fl oz) olive oil

410 g (13 oz) tomatoes, blanched, peeled and diced

3-4 cloves garlic, diced

5 g (1 teaspoon) sugar

5 g (1 teaspoon) cayenne pepper

5 g (1 teaspoon) finely chopped fresh basil

10 g (2 teaspoons) dried oregano

Freshly ground black pepper

90 mL (3 fl oz) vinegar

*Since black-eyed beans can be very dry, it is best to serve them with a little sauce such as this aromatic and piquant version.*

In a pan, heat the oil and sauté the tomatoes for 5–10 minutes until soft. Stir in all the other ingredients except the vinegar.

Simmer on low heat stirring regularly, for 20–30 minutes until the sauce has thickened. Remove from the heat, stand for 3–5 minutes and stir in the vinegar. Cool and set aside or serve hot with black-eyed beans, plantains or boiled rice.

SERVES 6–8

## CUBA

Discovered during his first voyage to the region in 1492, Columbus at first thought he had reached China. This did not deter him from naming the island 'Juana' in honour of the daughter of his patrons, Ferdinand and Isabella of Spain. The name was later changed to Santiago, favoured in many areas of Spanish colonisation to honour their country's patron saint, but eventually reverted to Cuba, the name used by the island's original Arawak Indian inhabitants.

Cuba was colonised early, in 1511, and the Arawaks were enslaved and virtually died out within a few years. They were replaced, as so often happened in the history of the Caribbean islands, by slaves from West Africa. Despite this, unlike many of the other islands, the majority of Cuba's population is still dominated by those of European descent.

# CASUELA CRIOLA
CREOLE CASSEROLE

150 mL (¼ pt) vegetable oil

250 g (½ lb) pigs' trotters or 1 cup giblets, or 4 large portions (e.g. Maryland) chicken

2 onions, diced

4 cloves garlic diced

4 small red chillies (hot peppers)

4 large tomatoes, blanched, peeled and diced

10 g (2 teaspoons) oregano

5 mL (1 teaspoon) mushroom or soya sauce

2 L (3½ pt) water

2 bay leaves

5 g (1 teaspoon) salt

125 g (4 oz) red kidney beans, parboiled and drained

250 g (½ lb) each potatoes, sweet potatoes, yams and pumpkin, peeled and diced

1 ripe plantain or banana, peeled, ends trimmed off and cut into 6 rounds

Salt and pepper to taste

60-75 g (4-5 table-spoons) cornflour (cornstarch) blended with 150 mL (¼ pt) water

*This recipe is like a little beacon linking my homeland to Cuba. In Ghana it has always been a clever and delicious way to use up unattractive parts of meat or poultry or recycle leftovers, but I suspect during the era of slavery poor cuts of meat were the only ones available to blacks. This recipe, however, has travelled through generations of black Cuban families and has been much improved along the way.*

In a large cooking pot, heat the oil and sauté the pigs' trotters, giblets or chicken with the onions, garlic, chillies (hot peppers), tomatoes, oregano, and mushroom or soya sauce for about 10 minutes. Add the water, bay leaves and salt. Cook over low to medium heat until the meat is just tender. just tender.

Add the kidney beans and cook for 10–15 minutes. At 10 minute intervals, add the potatoes, then the yams, then the pumpkin and the plantain or banana last. Simmer on low heat for a further 10 minutes. Ajust the seasoning then mix in the blended cornflour (cornstarch). Simmer for a further 20–30 minutes.

Remove from the heat and skim off the excess oil, then serve hot with warm bread, boiled white rice or by itself. This filling dish makes an excellent winter soup.

*Note:* During the cooking process, try not to overstir the dish as it makes it more attractive when all the vegetables are recognisable at the end.

SERVES 4–6

**From New Orleans** Fish in Socks (page 149)

**From New Orleans** Corn Bread (page 156)

# MOROS Y CRISTIANOS
### MOORS AND CHRISTIANS

**250 g (½ lb) raw black-eyed beans soaked overnight in water**

**10 g (2 teaspoons) salt**

**1 large onion, diced**

**2 cloves garlic, diced**

**90 mL (3 fl oz) olive oil**

**250 g (½ lb) long-grain rice**

**500 mL (¾ pt) water from parboiling**

**Salt and pepper to taste**

**Fried plantains for serving (page 146)**

*The literal translation of this is 'Moors and Christians' and comes from the colour mix of the dark beans and white rice. Moors are Muslims of mixed Berber and Arab descent, many of whom live in Morocco in north-west Africa.*

*While this is another dish originating in Africa (where it is sometimes called 'Waatse' — pronounced 'wah-chay'), it has travelled west with the African people. In Cuba it is served with fried plantains, called Platanos Fritas (page 146), just as it is in Ghana and other West African states.*

Drain the soaked black-eyed beans and rinse in cold water. Fill up a large saucepan with about 1 L (1¾ pt) fresh water and add the salt. Parboil the beans for 20–30 minutes until they are semi-hard, not too soft. Remove the beans from the heat and drain off the water. Save both the bean water and the beans.

In a large cooking pot, sauté the onion and garlic in the olive oil until they begin to brown. Add the rice with 500 mL (¾ pt) reserved bean water. If there is more than 500 mL save the rest for later. Stir well, adjust the seasoning and simmer for 10–15 minutes on low heat.

Stir in the parboiled beans and add the rest of the bean water (if any) or more water seasoned with a little salt if the rice is too dry. Cook slowly on very low heat, checking frequently for water content. When the beans and rice are both soft and well done, serve hot, topped with fried plantains (page 146). This can be eaten alone or served as an accompaniment to stews and roasts with gravy.

SERVES 4

# PLATANOS FRITAS
## FRIED PLANTAINS

**3–4 whole ripe plantains (unripe is green; ripe is yellow)**

**Salt and pepper to taste**

**Vegetable oil for deep-frying**

*Although part of the same family as bananas, plantains (Musa spientum) cannot be eaten raw by humans; they need to be cooked first. In good company with beans, cassava, onions, tomatoes, sweet potatoes, corn (maize) and spinach (silver beet), plantains have travelled widely among the black communities of the world! There is a myriad of recipes for plantain, but this is one of the simplest.*

Trim off both ends of each plantain with a knife. Score firmly, but not too deeply, vertically from one end of the plantain to the other. Remove the skin.

There are many styles of cutting plantains, from the fancy to the plain depending on whom you want to please — yourself or others. I suggest you start with a simple style and evolve your own later.

Lay the peeled plantain on a chopping board, holding it firmly at one end. Starting from just above the furthest end, cut off thick portions diagonally until each piece has been cut up (approximately 6 portions per plantain). Sprinkle with salt and pepper and toss together. It is better to make the portions thicker to start with, as they are easier to turn while cooking.

Heat the oil in a deep-fryer. When very hot but not boiling, gently fry plantain portions until golden brown on both sides. Lift out, drain, set aside and keep hot. Serve with the dish of your choice. With roasted groundnuts (peanuts), this becomes a wonderful snack.

*Note:* As a variation, peel 2–3 ripe plantains in the same way, and cut them into thick 2 cm (1 in) vertical strips, cubed or cut into rounds. Season with a blended mixture of 2 fresh red chillies (hot peppers), 1 small piece of root ginger (grated), a pinch of salt and 125 mL (4 fl oz) water. Drain and deep-fry. Serve as a snack or with boiled beans or nuts. This variation is also very popular in West Africa, where it is sold on street corners at night.

SERVES 4

# PASTEL DE BATATA
### SWEET POTATO CAKE

60 mL (4 tablespoons) ginger wine or rum mixed with 125 mL (4 fl oz) water

Few drops vanilla essence

250 g (½ lb) sugar

500 g (1 lb) sweet potato, peeled, boiled and mashed

125 g (4 oz) butter, melted

3 eggs

125 g (4 oz) plain flour

Salt to taste

10 g (2 teaspoons) baking powder

*There are different types of sweet potatoes which range from the purple-skinned variety to the orange-skinned and the white-skinned varieties, depending on where they grow in the tropics.*

Combine the ginger wine, vanilla and sugar. Mix it into the sweet potato with the butter. Separate the egg yolks from the whites, beat the yolks well and add to the sweet potato.

Sift the flour, salt and baking powder together and fold into the sweet potato mix. Beat the egg whites until they form stiff peaks. Fold into the sweet potato and pour into a deep, lightly greased cake tin. Bake for 45 minutes to 1 hour in an oven preheated to 180°C (350°F). Check with a skewer after 40 minutes to see if the cake is cooked.

When cooked, remove from the heat, stand for 10–15 minutes then turn out onto a wire rack. Slice and serve as you wish with custard or cream.

SERVES 4

# LOUISIANA/NEW ORLEANS

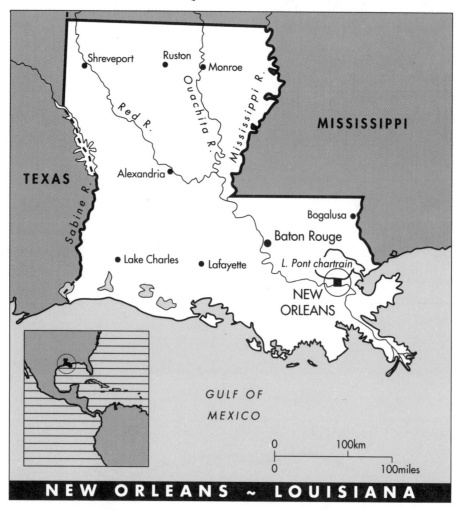

Shreveport · Ruston · Monroe · Red R. · Ouachita R. · Mississippi R. · MISSISSIPPI · TEXAS · Sabine R. · Alexandria · Baton Rouge · Bogalusa · Lake Charles · Lafayette · L. Pont chartrain · NEW ORLEANS · GULF OF MEXICO

0    100km
0    100miles

## NEW ORLEANS ~ LOUISIANA

**Status**    A southern state of the United States of America

**Capital city**    New Orleans

**Official language**    English

**Currency**    Dollar (US$) = 100 cents

**Total land area**    Approximately 126,000 sq km

New Orleans is not only Louisiana's capital but also a major sea port, located as it is on the Mississippi and with access to the Gulf of Mexico. The city is famous for the continued French flavour of its streetlife and nightlife, as are the annual Mardi Gras, and the jazz and blues tradition dating from the nineteenth century.

# FISH IN SOCKS

16 fish tails, each about 5 cm (2 in) long with some flesh on them

125 mL (4 fl oz) corn oil

*BATTER MIX*

125 g (4 oz) plain flour

10 g (2 teaspoons) mustard powder

5 g (1 teaspoon) paprika

2.5 g (½ teaspoon) salt

15 mL (1 tablespoon) spicy red ketchup

5 mL (1 teaspoon) Worcestershire sauce

5 mL (1 teaspoon) mayonnaise

125 mL (4 fl oz) lager or beer

5 mL (1 teaspoon) lemon juice

1 egg

5 g (1 teaspoon) finely chopped gherkin

1 small onion, very finely diced

*Considering that Creole ancestry is grounded in fish-eating West Africa, it is not surprising that fish features prominently in Creole cooking. The exciting thing about Creole cuisine is how the traditional African recipes have evolved with the French, Spanish, Portuguese and American Indian influences.*

*While the choice of fish for this recipe depends on local and seasonal availability, it is best to choose a fleshy variety with few bones.*

*Fish in Socks (or Fried Fish Tails in Batter) is a clever and tasty way to use the commonly leftover tail ends of a fish.*

Clean the fish tails and dry them on paper towels. In a mixing bowl, combine all the ingredients for the batter and stir well.

Heat the corn oil in a small saucepan until hot but not boiling. Dip each fish tail in batter, making sure you coat the whole piece. Gently shake off excess batter before frying in the hot oil until crisp and brown all over.

Remove from heat and drain on paper towels. Set aside and keep warm until all the fish tails are cooked. Serve hot as an appetiser or snack with a small, crisp salad.

SERVES 4

# DRUNKEN YABBIES

4 big yabbies or blue crabs, uncooked

500 mL (¾ pt) white wine or beer

500 mL (¾ pt) fish stock (see Note) or 1 fish stock cube crushed in equal quantity of hot water

2 cloves garlic, crushed

2 teaspoons chopped fennel, dill or chives

1 onion, quartered

3 tomatoes, blanched and peeled

1 red capsicum (sweet or bell pepper) seeded and quartered

20 g (4 teaspoons) sugar

10 g (2 teaspoons) unsalted butter

Salt and freshly ground black pepper to taste

10–20g (2–4 teaspoons) cornflour (cornstarch) mixed with 90 mL (3 fl oz) water

*Yabbies or blue crabs are a favourite with many coastal and island cultures in the Caribbean region. This particular recipe has a Louisiana Creole touch. The Louisiana Creoles are of Spanish and French origin and their cooking reflects their heritage. They like stylishly presented food, frequently cooked with wine.*

Bring plenty of water to boil in a large saucepan. Quickly drop in the yabbies or crabs, cover and simmer on high heat for 10–15 minutes. Remove from the heat, drain and rinse thoroughly in cold water. Put the yabbies or crabs back in the now-empty saucepan, add the wine or beer, and all the ingredients except the seasoning and the cornflour (cornstarch) mixed with water.

Bring to the boil and cook for 20–30 minutes or until all the ingredients are cooked.

Remove from the heat. Take out the yabbies or crabs, arrange them in an ovenproof dish, and cook in an oven preheated to 180°C (350°F) for approximately 30 minutes. Pour the sauce and vegetable mix into a blender and blend until smooth. Season to taste. Add the cornflour (cornstarch) mix, return to the saucepan and slowly stir on low heat until the sauce starts to thicken. Reduce the heat and cook for 1–2 minutes. Remove from the heat and pour the sauce over the crabs, sprinkle with herbs and serve hot with crusty French bread and fresh salad.

*Note:* To make your own fish stock, buy a variety of fish heads, wings, tails, crab or yabbie carcasses, claws, etc, from the fishmongers. Clean, put in a saucepan with 1 coarsely chopped, washed but unpeeled onion, 4 crushed garlic cloves, a handful of peppercorns, a lemon rind, 1 stick of celery, chopped, 2 L (3½ pt) water, 1 bay leaf, a sprig of parsley and a pinch of salt. Boil slowly on low heat for about 40 minutes to 1 hour. Stand for about 30 minutes, strain, discard solids and save the fish stock.

SERVES 4

# GUMBO

185 g (6 oz) unsalted butter

60 g (4 tablespoons) cornflour (cornstarch)

125 g (4 oz) onions, diced

3 cloves garlic, crushed

125 g (4 oz) green capsicum (sweet or bell pepper), diced

250 g (½ lb) celery, chopped

500 g (1 lb) okro (okra), sliced

500 g (1 lb) tomatoes, blanched, peeled and diced

500 g (1 lb) green (uncooked) prawns (shrimp)

4 small crayfish or crab claws, uncooked, with meat inside

4 roasted or fried chicken wings, halved

5 g (1 teaspoon) dried oregano or marjoram

1–2 bay leaves

2 chicken stock cubes in 1L (1¾ pt) water

250 g (½ lb) smoked ham or spicy pork sausage, diced

5 g (1 teaspoon) ground nutmeg

Salt and pepper to taste

15–30 g (1-2 tablespoons) gumbo filé (see Note)

1 kg (2 lb) long-grain rice, boiled

With the increasing popularity of Cajun and Creole cuisine the world over, Gumbo hardly needs an introduction. A thick soup made from okro (okra), crab, spicy sausage, chicken and spices, and laden with boiled rice, it looks like a watery risotto. It is usually served in a deep soup dish rather than a bowl and you will get maximum pleasure from eating it with a spoon and your fingers!

Like many other recipes to be found in the Caribbean region, there is an uncanny resemblance between the westernised and cosmopolitan Louisiana Gumbos and traditional West African okro (okra) and rice stews and soups, but with some regional and cultural changes.

In a large saucepan, make a roux by melting the butter, then blending in the cornflour (cornstarch). Stir well on medium heat for 5–10 minutes until light brown. Add the onions, garlic, capsicum (sweet or bell pepper), celery and okro (okra) to the roux and fry for 10 minutes. Add the tomatoes and prawns (shrimp) and cook for a further 5–10 minutes on low heat, taking care not to burn. Add the crayfish or crab claws, chicken pieces, oregano or marjoram, bay leaves and stock. Cook for about 20 minutes. Add the smoked ham, or sausage, and nutmeg. Stir well, season to taste, cover and simmer for another 20 minutes.

Lower the heat, and mix the gumbo filé separately into a smooth, runny paste with an equal amount of warm water and a small portion of strained sauce from the cooking pan. Add the gumbo filé paste to the sauce.

To serve, scoop boiled rice into the bottom of a big bowl. Arrange chicken, crab, ham and prawns (shrimp) with a generous portion of the gumbo sauce on top. Serve hot.

Note: Gumbo filé is often the secret ingredient in gumbo. It is powdered okro (okra) mixed with seasonings and thickening agents and thickens the gumbo sauce. Once added, stir on very low heat for 3–5 minutes.

SERVES 4–6

# MARDI GRAS

Mardi Gras — or versions such as Carnival or Val Val — is celebrated on most of the islands and regions to which African slaves were introduced.

Most of the preparations take place between the New Year and the beginning of Lent, culminating on 'Fat Tuesday', the day before Ash Wednesday. Originally the festival was held by the plantation owners and European colonisers who amalgamated their own festivities, such as the Shrove Tuesday end to the Lenten Festival in France, with those rituals they had observed amongst their slave labourers.

The main attraction of the New Orleans Mardi Gras is the enormous parade of floats, each sponsored by a 'Krewe', traditionally secret groups from which African, Jewish and Asian-born residents were excluded. From amongst the Krewes a Krewe King and Queen are selected to ride on the royal float. These roles have in the past conferred great social status on the chosen pair. The King and Queen and their entourage are richly dressed and, as part of the ritual, throw masses of junk jewellery mixed with valuable, specially minted coins to the crowds massed along the streets.

Following the Krewe Parade are the 'alternative' floats, created in parody by the black community. This time the King and Queen wear Zulu dress, complete with leopard skins, and are attended by a Zulu entourage including a witch doctor and a 'Big Shot' character who represents the wealth of Africa. Instead of gilt and coins, the Zulu King's entourage throws coconuts to the crowd.

It is fascinating to note that most African tribal festivals in West Africa, such as the Ghanaian Ga people's 'Homowo', the Ewe's 'hogbotsotsu' and the 'Corn and Cassava' festival in Benin, culminate in parades of fetish priests and priestesses, and are held on a Tuesday, just like Mardi Gras.

# HONEYED ROAST LEG OF PORK

**Vegetable oil for baking**

**1.5–2 kg (3–4 lb) leg of pork with the skin heavily scored in a criss-cross fashion**

**8–10 whole cloves**

**15 g (1 tablespoon) cornflour (cornstarch)**

**10 g (2 teaspoons) cayenne powder**

**10 g (2 teaspoons) ground cinnamon**

**5 g (1 teaspoon) salt**

**15 mL (1 tablespoon) honey**

**3 cooking apples, peeled, cored and quartered**

*It is probable that pork was introduced into the diet of the Spanish Creoles of Louisiana by the Arcadians/Cajuns or the Creoles' black slaves. This particular recipe probably came to Louisiana from the West Indies where the African slaves would have learnt to combine sweet and savoury ingredients in a single dish – a practice that occurred only rarely in Africa itself.*

*Honeyed Roast Leg of Pork is served as a celebratory dish.*

Place the oil and leg of pork in a baking dish and stick cloves firmly in between the scores in the skin, pushing them into the flesh underneath. Mix together the cornflour (cornstarch), cayenne, cinnamon and salt. Rub meat all over with the cornflour mix, making sure to season between the scores in the skin, too.

Bake uncovered in an oven pre-heated to 200°C (400°F) for approximately 30 minutes. Turn the meat over and bake the other side for another 30 minutes. Remove the meat from the baking dish. Drain the oil from the dish and return the meat to the dish with the top of the leg uppermost. Smear honey all over the meat. Arrange the apples around the pork in the baking dish. Lower heat to medium, 180°C (350°F), cover and continue baking for another hour. Uncover the meat, turn up heat slightly to 190°C (375°F) and brown for 25–30 more minutes until meat is well cooked, tender and brown.

Serve with potato croquettes and vegetables roasted with the meat during the last 30–45 minutes of baking time.

*Note:* As a guide, allow 25–30 minutes of baking time per 500 g (1 lb) of meat plus an extra 25–30 minutes for browning (eg: 1.5 kg (3 lb) leg of pork should take 1 hour 15 minutes to 1 hour 30 minutes plus browning time.

SERVES 6–8

# DIRTY RICE

125 g (4 oz) chicken livers, diced

125 g (4 oz) chicken hearts, diced

125 g (4 oz) chicken or turkey gizzards, skinned and diced

6 chicken wings, halved to make 12 small pieces

15 g (1 tablespoon) each ground nutmeg and garlic powder, combined with a pinch of salt and 30 g (2 tablespoons) plain flour

1 L (1¾ pt) chicken stock or 1 chicken stock cube crushed into same quantity of boiling water

1 bay leaf

6 cloves garlic, crushed

Salt to taste

Dash each Tabasco and Worcestershire sauces

250 mL (8 fl oz) vegetable oil or bacon dripping

4 onions, diced

3 red chillies (hot peppers), diced (optional)

250 g (½ lb) tomatoes, blanched, peeled and diced

375 g (¾ lb) long-grain rice

10 g (2 teaspoons) finely chopped fresh oregano

5 g (1 teaspoon) freshly ground black pepper

*This is Cajun food at its grass roots best. Hearty, inexpensive and wholesome, it is served everywhere that Cajun cooking is served. Dirty Rice is actually a concoction of leftovers and, despite the name, the finished product is finger-licking good and looks 'mighty fine' when served with flair.*

Pat the meat dry with paper towels then place in a big bowl and season with the nutmeg, garlic powder, salt and flour mix. Pour 250 mL (8 fl oz) stock into a saucepan. Add the bay leaf, half the garlic, a dash of salt and all the meat. Bring to the boil, lower the heat and simmer until meat is cooked. Remove the bay leaf. Set aside to cool for 20 minutes. In a blender or food processor, blend livers, hearts and gizzards to a rough paste. Add Tabasco and Worcestershire sauces and set aside.

In a very large saucepan, heat the oil or dripping and fry the seasoned chicken wings until nearly brown. Remove from the oil, drain and set aside. In the same oil, fry the onions, chillies (hot peppers) and remaining garlic for about 5 minutes, on low heat, without browning the onions. Add the tomatoes and stir well. Cook for 3–4 minutes. Add the rice, oregano, black pepper, blended offal, chicken wings and remaining chicken stock. Stir well to mix, season to taste, lower the heat and cook for about 30–40 minutes or until all the liquid is absorbed and the rice and meat are soft and cooked.

Serve hot on a bed of fresh greens, garnished with hard-boiled eggs and/or fresh tomatoes, chives, black olives and sliced matchstick carrots.

SERVES 6–8

# VEGETABLE HERB BAKE

5 large eggs

90 g (3 oz) fresh spinach (silver beet), very finely sliced

90 g (3 oz) fresh carrots, grated

1 small capsicum (sweet or bell pepper) seeded and, diced

90 g (3 oz) fresh chives

1 tablespoon finely chopped fresh basil

1 tablespoon finely chopped fresh dill

60 g (4 tablespoons) self-raising flour

Salt and freshly ground black pepper to taste

185 g (6 oz) grated cheddar or gouda cheese

1 tablespoon finely chopped fresh coriander (cilantro)

90 g (3 oz) fresh broad-leafed parsley

*Folks from Louisiana waste nothing if they can help it, so all leftovers are recycled into evermore delicious recipes. This all-vegetable recipe goes well with the 'King of Gumbos' served on Good Fridays in Southern Louisiana. The King of Gumbos adds freshly bought green vegetables to the traditional Gumbo recipe (page 151).*

Break the eggs, separate the whites from the yolks and set aside both. Combine the egg yolks and the vegetables, chives, basil and dill and flour together in a large bowl. Mix well together. Check seasoning and adjust accordingly. Whisk egg whites in a separate bowl until stiff peaks form. Using a wooden spoon, first stir two spoonfuls of egg whites into the vegetable mixture. Fold the remaining whisked egg white into the mixture, taking care to work from the sides of the bowl towards the centre, to maintain the lightness of the mixture. Season to taste.

Grease a ring baking dish and pour the mixture carefully into it. Scatter the grated cheese evenly over the top. Bake in an oven pre-heated to 180–190°C (350–375°F) for 35–40 minutes or until the dish is cooked through the centre and brown on the edges. Remove from the heat and stand for 10 minutes. Cover the dish with a large, flat plate and turn it upside-down. Fill the centre with fresh coriander (cilantro) leaves or parsley. Serve hot with a fresh, crisp, green salad and some Garlic Sauce (page 59) or with Gumbo (page 151).

SERVES 4

# CORNBREAD

250 g (½ lb) yellow
cornmeal or polenta

250 g (½ lb) plain flour

15 g (1 tablespoon) baking
powder

60 g (2 oz) sugar

5 g (1 teaspoon) salt

1 egg, beaten

250 mL (8 fl oz) milk

60 g (2 oz) butter, melted

*Cornbread has been around for about as long as the 'Deep South' of America has. It is a crumbly, gritty, semi-sweet mixture of baked cornmeal, eggs, butter and sugar. Delicious when served hot with stews, or just buttered and eaten warm with sweet pickles or jam, it is a favourite in Cajun/Creole cuisine. There are a variety of ways to make it, with room for individual touches.*

Combine all the dry ingredients in a mixing bowl. Make a well in the centre and pour in the egg and milk and whisk for 1 minute. Fold in the melted butter.

Grease a loaf tin and pour in the mixture. Bake in the middle of an oven preheated to 180°C (350°F) for 30–40 minutes or until cooked. Remove from the oven and stand for 10 minutes before turning out onto a wire rack. Serve sliced and buttered.

MAKES 1 LOAF

# GLOSSARY

**ablémamu**   roasted ground corn

**ackee**   edible fruit (when cooked) of seed pods of *Blighia sapida*, a tree common to Africa and the Caribbean. Available fresh or tinned

**apem**   baby plantain

**aportoryiwa (Ghana)**   a round earthenware bowl of the Akan tribe

**banku (Ghana)**   cornmeal dumpling

**berberé (Ethiopia)**   a dry spice seasoning

**cajun**   a person born in Louisiana and descended from the French exiles of Acadia in Canada

**callaloo**   a green-leafed plant used as a form of spinach in the West Indies

**capsicum**   sweet or bell pepper

**chilli**   hot pepper

**chinchin**   sweet West African dough balls

**cocoyam**   taro

**coriander**   cilantro

**corn**   yellow maize

**cornflour**   cornstarch

**couscous**   durum wheat grains

**cream**   single cream

**creole**   originally those of European (particularly French and Spanish) descent born in the West Indies, Spanish America or the southern United States. Also a person born in the West Indies or Spanish America and descended from African slaves. Also a person of mixed European and African ancestry in those places

**dasheen**   a term by which varieties of 'spinach' are known in some Caribbean countries

**dênde oil (Brazil)**   palm oil

**eggplant**   aubergine

**egushi**   pumpkin seeds. Also known as pepitas

**eta (Ghana)**   flat-ended Ashanti wooden masher

**fufu**   a variety of dumpling frequently made from root vegetables. Also known as foofoo in the West Indies

**fuul medames**   a variety of brown broadbean, particularly popular in Egypt in a dish of the same name

**gari**   coarse cassava powder. Also known as manioc or in Brazil as farinhe de mandioca and in French-speaking countries as farine de manioc

**groundnuts**   peanuts

**gumbo**   a thick soup or stew, generally containing okro (okra) amongst many other ingredients, and popular in Africa, the Caribbean and the southern United States

**gungo peas**   Jamaican term for pigeon peas

**hamine eggs**   eggs boiled in their shells in stew or soups to take up the colour and flavour. Popular in Egypt

**jollof**   a West African risotto

**kaawé**   traditional African cooking (meat tenderising) stone

**kenkey**   wrapped cornmeal dumpling (general term)

**komi (Ghana)**   corn dumpling (Ga regional terminology)

**kontomiré**   leaves of the cocoyam (taro) plant

**kubécake**   West African coconut rum balls.

**loo (Ghana)**   fish or meat (Ga regional terminology)

**manioc**   coarse cassava powder. Also known as gari in West Africa, farinhe de mandioca in Brazil and farine de manioc in French-speaking countries

**makhrata**   Egyptian double-handed metal chopper

**mashamba**   a local variety of Zimbabwean pumpkin

**mealie meal**   Southern African thickened corn porridge

**mchicha**   leafy plant similar to spinach (silver beet), a staple food in Tanzania

**mitmita (Ethiopia)**   a variety of yellow pepper

**moi-moi**   Nigerian savoury bean paté

**okro**   okra

**pepita**   pumpkin seed. Also known as egushi

**plantain**   a member of the banana family. Should only be eaten when cooked. Best used unripened

**pawpaw**   papaya

**rapoko**   red millet flour

**sadza (Zimbabwe)**   white maize or millet dumpling

**shallots**   spring onions

**shitor (Ghana)**   chilli sambal

**snow peas**   mange tout

**spinach**   silver beet. Also a generic term used for different edible green leaves of plants indigenous to various African or Caribbean countries, such as callaloo, dasheen, etc

**thickened cream**   double cream

**wot**   Ethiopian stew

**zucchini**   courgette

# BIBLIOGRAPHY

The Africa Review (The Economic and Business Report) 1991–92 (15th ed.), Hunter Publishing Inc. Edison, N.J.

The Americas Review (The Economic and Business Report) 1991–92 (12th ed.), Hunter Publishing, Inc., Edison, NJ

Barrett, Leonard, The Sun and The Drum, Sangster's Book Stores in association with Heinemann Educational Books, Kingston, 1976

Bennett, Olivia, Village In Egypt, A & C Black (Publishers) Ltd, London, 1983

Chesi, Gert, The Last Africans (3rd ed.), Perlinger Verlag, Wörgl, Austria, 1981

Chesi, Gert, Voodoo Africa's Secret Power (2nd ed.), Perlinger Verlag, Wörgl, Austria, 1981

Crowder, Michael, West Africa Under Colonial Rule, Hutchinson and Co. (Publishers) Ltd, London, 1968

Crowther, Geoff, Africa On A Shoestring (5th ed.) Lonely Planet Publications, Victoria, 1989

ESN — Nutrition Country Profile, FAO (Food and Agricultural Organisation), United Nations, 1986–1990

Fisher, Angela, Africa Adorned, William Collins Sons & Co Ltd, London 1984

Hultman, Tami (ed.), The Africa News Cookbook, Viking Penguin Inc., New York, 1985

New Secondary Atlas For Tanzania, Longman Group UK Ltd, Essex, 1988

Outline Series 1988–1991 (ISBN 08 10–2384), Department of Foreign Affairs and Trade, Australia

Porter, Darwin (assisted by Danforth Prince), Frommer's Caribbean 92, Prentice Hall, New York 1992

Uhl, Michael, Frommer's Rio 1989–90, New York, Prentice Hall, 1989

# INDEX OF RECIPES

18M